**New Directions for
Student Leadership**

Susan R. Komives
EDITOR-IN-CHIEF

Kathy L. Guthrie
ASSOCIATE EDITOR

Innovative Learning for Leadership Development

Julie E. Owen

EDITOR

Number 145 • Spring 2015
Jossey-Bass
San Francisco

INNOVATIVE LEARNING FOR LEADERSHIP DEVELOPMENT
Julie E. Owen (ed.)
New Directions for Student Leadership, No. 145, Spring 2015

Susan R. Komives, Editor-in-Chief
Kathy L. Guthrie, Associate Editor

Microfilm copies of issues and articles are available in 16mm and 35mm, as well as microfiche in 105mm, through University Microfilms Inc., 300 North Zeeb Road, Ann Arbor, MI 48106-1346.

New Directions for Student Leadership is indexed in Academic Search Alumni Edition (EBSCO Publishing), Education Index/Abstracts (EBSCO Publishing), ERA: Educational Research Abstracts Online (T&F), ERIC: Educational Resources Information Center (CSC), MLA International Bibliography (MLA).

NEW DIRECTIONS FOR STUDENT LEADERSHIP (ISSN 2373-3349, electronic ISSN 2373-3357) is part of the Jossey-Bass Higher and Adult Education Series and is published quarterly by Wiley Subscription Services, Inc., A Wiley Company, at Jossey-Bass, One Montgomery Street, Suite 1200, San Francisco, CA 94104-4594. POSTMASTER: Send all address changes to New Directions for Student Leadership, Jossey-Bass, One Montgomery Street, Suite 1200, San Francisco, CA 94104-4594.

SUBSCRIPTIONS for print only: $89.00 for individuals in the U.S./Canada/Mexico; $113.00 international. For institutions, agencies, and libraries, $342.00 U.S.; $382.00 Canada/Mexico; $416.00 international. Electronic only: $89.00 for individuals all regions; $342.00 for institutions all regions. Print and electronic: $98.00 for individuals in the U.S., Canada, and Mexico; $122.00 for individuals for the rest of the world; $411.00 for institutions in the U.S.; $451.00 for institutions in Canada and Mexico; $485.00 for institutions for the rest of the world. Prices subject to change. Refer to the order form that appears at the back of most volumes of this journal.

EDITORIAL CORRESPONDENCE should be sent to the Associate Editor, Kathy L. Guthrie, at kguthrie@fsu.edu.

Cover design: Wiley
Cover Images: © Lava 4 images | Shutterstock

www.josseybass.com

Contents

1. Transforming Leadership Development for Significant Learning   7
Julie E. Owen

Leadership education is undergoing a transformation where powerful pedagogies and emerging knowledge about the scholarship of teaching and learning supplant long held and often-outmoded practices of leadership education. This transformation requires new commitments to evidence-based practice, critical consciousness, and more complex understanding of the levers of leadership learning.

2. Building Critical Capacities for Leadership Learning   19
Mark Anthony Torrez, Melissa L. Rocco

Cognitive elements of transformational learning, particularly metacognition and critical self-reflection, are discussed as essential considerations for leadership development in the 21st century. The importance of developmentally sequencing leadership-learning experiences and addressing evolving complexities of leadership identity are also explored.

3. Navigating Leadership Complexity Through Critical, Creative, and Practical Thinking   35
Jennifer M. Pigza

Leadership education that intentionally addresses critical, creative, and practical thinking enhances significant learning for students and deepens the leadership practices of educators. This chapter explores specific applications in the areas of graduate leadership education, action research, service immersion program, and advising conversations. Additionally, it presents a framework of pathways to social change and suggests how such a framework can be useful to students and leadership educators.

4. Integrative and Interdisciplinary Approaches to Leadership Development   49
Julie E. Owen

Integrating diverse conceptions of leadership across different disciplines, perspectives, and epistemologies is imperative if leaders are to operate in a global and networked world. Interdisciplinary and integrative leadership courses and digital learning communities are featured examples.

SERIES EDITORS' NOTES

Since the 1990s, the field of leadership education has broadened, deepened, and focused. Nearly every academic field of study recognizes that students need to assume leadership roles in their jobs, professions, families, local communities, and in a shared world community. Professional associations that accredit college degree fields commonly include leadership capacity as a required outcome of the college experience (Seemiller, 2013; Sharp, Komives, & Fincher, 2011) and nearly every college proclaims a goal of their graduates being civically engaged global leaders. Although high school curricula are more prescribed than college curricula and often do not allow space for leadership coursework, school- and non-school-based leadership experiences exist in every school district to promote youth leadership development (Klau, Boyd, Luckow, & Associates, 2006; Komives & Dugan, 2014) and there is a growing body of knowledge about youth leadership development (Murphy & Reichard, 2011). We find it encouraging that the scholarship in leadership development recognizes diverse contexts and diversity among students (Guthrie, Bertrand Jones, Osteen, & Hu, 2013).

This is not to say, however, that those valuing or even teaching leadership have a professional grounding in leadership as a field of study, yet more and more educators in these recent decades have added leadership expertise to their disciplinary focus or have become professional leadership educators. The professionalization of the leadership education field is evidenced by such developments as new professional associations, dedicated journals, student-centered textbooks and theoretical/conceptual models, substantial research and assessment, and standards of practice (Komives, 2011). Undergraduates at thousands of colleges and universities can enroll in curricular or cocurricular leadership certificate programs, academic minors, and even in major areas of study. Leadership educators can do specialization graduate work in various disciplines or in the field of leadership as their major area of study. This *New Directions for Student Leadership* series is part of that evolving picture that will further advance good practices and research on student leadership.

About This Series

This *New Directions for Student Leadership* series will explore dimensions of the development of leadership in high school youth and college students of all ages to aid leadership educators who design educational programs.

We offer gratitude and complements to the series editors for the *New Directions for Youth Development* series on their fine work for many years. That series included such issues as Klau et al.'s (2006) issue on *Youth Leadership*. Readers of that series will find a continued emphasis on applications of leadership applicable to high school students and youth, as well as the diverse range of college students in this series.

New Directions for Student Leadership premiers with this first issue on *Innovative Learning for Leadership Development* with issue editor Julie Owen from George Mason University. Subsequent issues, with their working titles, in this inaugural year and their editors include *Developing Ethical Leaders* (Arthur Schwartz, Widener University), *Student Leadership Development Through Recreation and Athletics* (Don Stenta, Ohio State University, and Cara McFadden, Elon College), and *Engagement and Leadership for Social and Political Change* (Kathleen Knight Abowitz and Michael Evans, Miami University Ohio). Subsequent issues will include such topics as leadership development through service learning and cross-cultural dimensions of leadership development, and proposals will be accepted on diverse topics related to high school and/or college student leadership development.

As editors of this series, we view leadership as philosophies, capacities, and identities that can be learned and developed by any person who wants to engage with others toward shared purposes. Leadership is also a process used when people come together and is manifest in organizations of all kinds. We have much to learn and much to teach each other about leadership in a variety of contexts, leadership for diverse learners, pedagogies and experiences for teaching and learning leadership, and applying research to leadership education. Our goal is to bring the best of recent thinking, best practices, and current challenges to the readers of this series who, in turn, will continue their quest to offer superb educational experiences to students to develop their leadership efficacy and leadership capacity. We invite you on this journey with us and welcome your feedback and ideas at any time.

Susan R. Komives
Editor

Kathy L. Guthrie
Associate Editor

References

Guthrie, K. L., Bertrand Jones, T., Osteen, L., & Hu, S. (2013). *Cultivating leader identity and capacity in students from diverse backgrounds* (ASHE Higher Education Report, 39[4]). San Francisco, CA: Jossey-Bass.

Klau, M., Boyd, S., Luckow, L., & Associates. (2006). Youth leadership. *New Directions for Youth Development: No. 109*. San Francisco, CA: Jossey-Bass.

Komives, S. R. (2011). Advancing leadership education. In S. R. Komives, J. P. Dugan, J. E. Owen, C. Slack, W. Wagner, & Associates (Eds.), *The handbook for student leadership development* (2nd ed., pp. 1–32). San Francisco, CA: Jossey-Bass.

Komives, S. R., & Dugan, J. P. (2014). Student leadership development: Theory, research, and practice. In D. Day (Ed.), *The Oxford handbook of leadership and organizations* (pp. 805–831). New York, NY: Oxford University Press.

Murphy, S. E. & Reichard, R. J. (Eds.) (2011). *Early development and leadership: Building the next generation of leaders*. New York, NY: Psychology Press.

Seemiller, C. (2013). *The student leadership competencies guidebook: Designing intentional leadership learning and development*. San Francisco, CA: Jossey-Bass.

Sharp, M. D., Komives, S. R., & Fincher, J. (2011). Learning outcomes in academic disciplines: Identifying common ground. *Journal of Student Affairs Research and Practice*, *48*, 481–504.

SUSAN R. KOMIVES *is professor emerita in the Student Affairs Graduate Program at the University of Maryland, co-founder of the National Clearinghouse for Leadership Programs, and co-author or co-editor of a dozen books including* Exploring Leadership, Handbook for Student Leadership Development, *and* Leadership for a Better World. *She is former co-principle investigator of the international Multi-Institutional Study of Leadership and the Leadership Identity Development model. She is the 2013 recipient of the Lifetime Achievement Award from ACPA: College Student Educator's International.*

KATHY L. GUTHRIE *is associate professor in higher education at Florida State University and coordinator of the Undergraduate Certificate in Leadership Studies. She has co-edited a* New Directions in Student Services *sourcebook titled* Developing Undergraduate Student Leadership Capacity *and recently co-authored* Cultivating Leader Identity and Capacity in Students from Diverse Backgrounds. *She serves on the editorial board for* Journal of Leadership Education, Journal of College and Character, *and* Journal of Student Affairs Research and Practice.

EDITOR'S NOTES

Leadership education is at a crossroads. Despite transformative texts such as *Leadership Can Be Taught* (Daloz Parks, 2005), *Deeper Learning in Leadership* (Roberts, 2007), and *Learning as a Way of Leading* (Preskill & Brookfield, 2009) many leadership practitioners continue to view themselves primarily as programmers, as providers of services and activities. This outlook can be especially detrimental to those working in the area of leadership development, which is increasingly calling for educators skilled in the creation of engaged pedagogy, integrative learning experiences, and intentional learning communities. As Roberts (2007) so eloquently states in *Deeper Learning in Leadership*,

> if deeper leadership is to unfold through, and as a result of, higher education, our intellectual and organizational models will have to be examined and radically altered so that all educators see themselves serving as leaders and key contributors to the learning process. (p. 209)

This volume draws on recent scholarship of teaching and learning in order to critically examine the intersections of learning and leadership.

How does what we know about the diversity of learners, learning styles, and the evolution of leadership identity shape how we foster leadership in students? What are important considerations in the design of transformational leadership learning environments? How do we encourage students to embrace the complexity of leadership theories and application? This volume invites readers to recognize the qualities and attributes of today's student learners, to develop a more complex understanding of the levers of leadership learning, to create environments that promote meaningful and measurable leadership learning, and to commit to evidence-based practice.

This volume puts forth the following suppositions: that leadership can and should be learned; that the learning and development leadership capacities are inextricably intertwined; and that leadership educators can purposefully foster learning environments that help students integrate knowledge, skills, and experiences in meaningful ways. Using L. Dee Fink's (2013) taxonomy of significant learning from the book *Creating Significant Learning Experiences* as a scaffold, experts in leadership education draw connections between emerging scholarship of teaching and learning and current trends in leadership. Additionally, this volume examines socialization to the role of leadership educator and the roles of authenticity (being true to one's self) and criticality in education (interrogating beliefs and questioning power dynamics). Select learning theories and their implications for leadership learning are presented. Strategies for constructing leadership-related learning outcomes and assessing leadership learning are also discussed. Examples and applications for high school and college students are included throughout this issue.

A brief note of thanks as a volume such as this does not come together without the wisdom and support of a large community of people. Profound gratitude to Susan Komives, Kathy Guthrie, Erin Null, Alison Knowles, Paul Foster, and the rest of the team at Jossey-Bass for making this series a possibility, and for committing the inaugural issue to the topic of innovations in leadership learning. Special thank-yous to John O'Connor, Lesley Smith, Kim Eby, Andrew Wingfield, Suzanne Scott, Paul Gorksi, Nance Lucas, Jeannie Brown Leonard, and the faculty in New Century College at George Mason University for teaching me the nuances of interdisciplinary and integrative education. You are guiding lights in fostering deliberative democracy and critical pedagogy. Finally, thank you to my "fictive kin"— Dugan, Garland, and Wendy—and my family near and far, especially Ken, Laura, Bennett, and Connie. I dedicate this volume to the memory of my father, Capt. Donald George Owen, a lifelong leader and learner.

Julie E. Owen
Editor

References

Daloz Parks, S. (2005). *Leadership can be taught*. Boston, MA: Harvard Business School Press.

Fink, L. D. (2013). *Creating significant learning experiences: An integrated approach to designing college courses* (2nd ed.). San Francisco, CA: Jossey-Bass.

Preskill, S., & Brookfield, S. D. (2009). *Learning as a way of leading: Lessons from the struggle for social justice*. San Francisco, CA: Jossey-Bass.

Roberts, D. C. (2007). *Deeper learning in leadership*. San Francisco, CA: Jossey-Bass.

JULIE E. OWEN *is an associate professor of leadership and integrative studies and executive director of Social Action & Integrative Learning (SAIL) in New Century College at George Mason University, where she teaches courses on socially responsible leadership, civic engagement, and community-based research. She is a scholar for the National Clearinghouse for Leadership Programs (NCLP) and is co-editor of both editions of the* Handbook for Student Leadership Development *(Jossey-Bass). She is a frequent presenter, consultant, and keynote speaker on topics related to leadership, social change, and organizational development. She is a 2005 recipient of AAC&U's K. Patricia Cross Future Leaders Award and a 2012 Mason Teaching Excellence Award winner.*

1

Leadership education is undergoing a transformation where powerful pedagogies and emerging knowledge about the scholarship of teaching and learning supplant long held and often-outmoded practices of leadership education. This transformation requires new commitments to evidence-based practice, critical consciousness, and more complex understanding of the levers of leadership learning.

Transforming Leadership Development for Significant Learning

Julie E. Owen

In his seminal article "Dysfunctional Illusions of Rigor," Craig Nelson (2010) interrogates many "common sense" adages about teaching and learning. Nelson (2010) describes his own transformational learning moment where he let go of long held beliefs about the sovereignty of course lectures and breadth of content in favor of engaged learning strategies and deep understanding. He states, "there were no deficits [in learning] that were not made irrelevant by appropriate pedagogy" (Nelson, 2010, p. 178). The field of leadership education needs a similar transformation where powerful pedagogies and emerging knowledge about the scholarship of teaching and learning supplant long held and often outmoded practices of leadership education. Such a shift would require new ways of thinking about leadership education, new commitments to evidence-based practice, and more complex understanding of the levers of leadership learning. Concurrently, practitioners of leadership may need to undergo a fundamental shift to start thinking of themselves as leadership educators.

This chapter examines the link between leadership and learning, introduces Fink's (2003, 2013) taxonomy of significant learning from the book *Creating Significant Learning Experiences* as a scaffold for the volume, discusses core competencies of leadership education, reviews existing supports for leadership programs, and ends with a challenge to leadership educators to become critical consumers and lifelong learners of leadership.

NEW DIRECTIONS FOR STUDENT LEADERSHIP, no. 145, Spring 2015 © 2015 Wiley Periodicals, Inc., A Wiley Company
Published online in Wiley Online Library (wileyonlinelibrary.com) • DOI: 10.1002/yd.20120

Linking Leadership and Learning

This volume connects important insights from the scholarship of teaching and learning to the practice of leadership education and development. There have been numerous prior efforts to ground leadership in learning (Daloz Parks, 2005; Day, Harrison, & Halpin, 2009; Preskill & Brookfield, 2009; Roberts, 2007; Vaill, 1998), yet many programs that claim to be developing student leaders still rely on leadership fads, reductionistic platitudes, and nondevelopmental approaches. Wide-reaching research programs on student leadership development, such as the *Multi-Institutional Study of Leadership* (MSL) which has surveyed over 300,000 participants, are revealing differential influences of educational environments in shaping leadership capacities and related variables such as efficacy, resilience, and cognitive skills (Dugan, Kodama, Correia, & Associates, 2013). However, few programs are applying these evidence-based practices, and more work is to be done to develop significant leadership learning. Exploring the lasting impact of leadership and learning in students' lives, Roberts (2007) states:

> I propose that deeper learning and deeper leadership are closely aligned, if not one and the same. Leadership capability is an important outcome of the higher education experience, but it is not the only or necessarily the most desirable outcome. As we look ever more closely at what we are achieving, there is emerging evidence that deeper learning is a necessary condition to foster deeper leadership. (p. 17)

If deeper or more lasting learning is a prerequisite for more meaningful and effective leadership, leadership educators must stay current on emerging findings from areas as diverse as cognitive science, motivation theory, metacognition (thinking about thinking), hermeneutics (making meaning), and critical scholarship. How adept are leadership educators at creating learning environments that value "attention, contribution, risk, evaluation, synthesis, application, empathy, and cooperation" (Bowen, 2012, p. 213)? The answers likely depend on one's perspective. For clarity, there are several suppositions about leadership and learning that weave throughout this volume and were noted in my Editor's Notes. These include the idea that leadership can and should be learned; that the learning and development of leadership capacities are inextricably intertwined; and that leadership educators can purposefully foster learning environments that help students integrate knowledge, skills, and experiences in meaningful ways. It should be said that there are approaches to leadership that may not agree with these suppositions, such as managerial theories that focus on leadership selection rather than leadership development and growth. Readers are invited to interrogate their own beliefs about the nature and purpose of leadership education throughout this volume.

Creating Significant Leadership Learning

Leadership educators have long seen the value of engaged pedagogy and active learning. Techniques such as case studies, debates, role-playing, problem-based learning, small group activities, simulations, and community engagement are frequently used tools in curricular, cocurricular, and community leadership development programs (Jenkins, 2012). The danger comes when educators apply these techniques with little regard to how they function as levers of learning, how they might apply differentially to students with diverse backgrounds and prior experiences, and with little thought about how intentionally to gauge learning in formative (i.e., during the process) and summative ways (at the end of the experience). For a long time, educators relied on Bloom's (1956) *Taxonomy of Educational Objectives* and Anderson and Krathwohl's (2001) subsequent revision to articulate levels of thinking present in learning processes. Bloom (1956) originally articulated learning in three separate domains—cognitive, affective, and psychomotor. In an effort to move beyond a hierarchical approach to knowledge acquisition and to promote more integrative learning experiences, Fink (2003, 2013) designed a taxonomy of significant learning that incorporates emerging principles of learning-centered design and integrates previously distinct domains of intellect, belief, and application. Fink posits six categories that promote significant learning, and each of these is addressed in this volume.

The first of Fink's (2013) categories, *foundational knowledge*, refers to learners *understanding and remembering specific information and ideas* core to any discipline of area of study. For leadership, there is an emerging canon of what constitutes core foundations of leadership studies (Bass, 1990; Northouse, 2012). Some of these leadership learning objectives that are articulated in the Council for the Advancement of Standards in Higher Education Standards for Student Leadership Programs are captured in Table 1.1, but there are numerous approaches (CAS, 2012). Leadership educators are typically well versed in Fink's second category of significant learning, *application*. Facilitating the ability of learners to connect theory to practice becomes essential to demonstrating the usefulness and relevance of leadership learning.

Fink's (2013) next category of significant learning involves the importance of *integration*, or making connections across ideas, people, and contexts. Chapter 4 of this volume posits that leaders must be educated in interdisciplinary, integrative, and intentional ways if they are to be effective in the networked world. Integration is essential to leadership education, especially as it relates to helping leaders develop a more holistic understanding of a problem or issue. Emerging data from the MSL refer to this ability as social perspective taking or the ability to see things from another's point of view (Dugan, Bohle, Woelker, & Cooney, 2014). Fink (2003) states, "the act

Table 1.1   Leadership Competencies Articulated in the Council for the Advancement of Standards (CAS) in Higher Education Student Leadership Program Standards

	Students Will Learn . . .
Foundations of leadership	• Historical perspectives on leaders, leadership, and leadership development • Established and evolving theoretical, conceptual, and philosophical frameworks of leadership • The distinction between management and leadership • Diverse approaches to leadership, including positional (leadership-follower dynamics) and nonpositional (collaborative-process models) • Theories and strategies of change • The integrative and interdisciplinary nature of leadership • Cross-cultural and global approaches to leadership
Personal development	• An awareness and understanding of various leadership styles and approaches • Exploration of a personal leadership philosophy, including personal values exploration, leadership identity development, and reflective practice • Connection of leadership to social identities and other dimensions of human development, such as psychosocial, cognitive, moral, and spiritual development • Leadership skill development, including accessing and critiquing sources of information, ethical reasoning and decision making, oral and written communication skills, critical thinking and problem solving, cultural competence, goal setting and visioning, motivation, creativity, and risk-taking
Interpersonal development	• Movement from dependent or independent to interdependent relationships • Development of self-efficacy for leadership • Recognition of the influences on leadership of multiple aspects of identity, such as race, gender identity and expression, sexual orientation, class, disability, nationality, religion, and ethnicity
The development of groups, organizations, and systems	• Team building • Developing trust • Group roles, group dynamics, and group development • Group problem solving, conflict management, and decision making • Shared leadership and collaboration

Table 1.1   Continued

Students Will Learn . . .
Organizational competencies: • Organizational planning, communication, and development • Organizational culture, values, and principles • Organizational politics and political systems • Organizational life cycles, sustainability, and stewardship • Methods of assessing and evaluating organizational effectiveness
Systems competencies: • Understanding and critiquing of systems and human behavior within systems, including functional and dysfunctional practices • Coalition-building and other methods of systemic change • Civic and community engagement • Leadership across diverse organizations, environments, and contexts

Source: From *CAS Professional Standards for Higher Education* (8th ed.). Copyright © 2012 Council for the Advancement of Standards in Higher Education. Reprinted with permission.

of making new connections gives learners a new form of power, especially intellectual power" (p. 31).

Chapter 5 addresses the next two categories of the taxonomy, *valuing the human dimensions of learning*, and *caring*. The field of leadership development has been at the forefront of integrating notions of emotional intelligence, personal and interpersonal competence, and authenticity with leadership development (Avolio, 2005; Goleman, 1995; Shankman, Allen, & Haber-Curran, in press), yet others still perceive these as "soft" or extraneous competencies. Fink (2003) argues that discovering the personal and social implications of learning can give students new views of themselves, new visions for future development and goals, and insights on how to interact more effectively with others. Fink (2013) states, "when students care about something, they then have the energy they need for learning more about it and making it part of their lives . . . without the energy for learning, nothing significant happens" (p. 32). In an era of increasing political disengagement and rapidly increasing awareness of crucial social problems, inspiring leaders who care may be the fundamental task of leadership educators.

The final category of Fink's (2013) taxonomy of significant learning is the importance of students *learning how to learn*. Chapter 2 in this volume examines the role of self-authorship and self-regulation in leadership learning. It connects processes of critical self-reflection, self-efficacy, resilience, adaptability, and motivation to leadership learning. The importance of developmentally sequencing leadership learning experiences, addressing evolving complexities of leadership identity, and developing metacognition is also explored. To Fink (2013), these processes are essential to creating lifelong learning and to enabling students to learn with greater effectiveness. As leadership is a rapidly evolving and ever changing set of skills, habits, knowledge, and capacities, these processes are fundamental.

Taken in total, Fink's (2013) taxonomy offers a roadmap to leadership educators about how to more intentionally ground leadership education in principles and practices of evidence-based learning. Practitioners can examine their leadership curricula, programs, and initiatives to see to what extent they are addressing each of Fink's domains. Unlike the hierarchical nature of Bloom's taxonomy, Fink (2013) posits that learning domains are interactive and relational in nature that results in a synergistic approach to learning. One can see how engaging student leaders in a service-learning project to apply learning to practice can also simultaneously promote caring and an appreciation for the human dimensions of leadership learning. The next section examines diverse articulations of what exactly is the foundational knowledge of leadership education and development.

Leadership Education Core Competencies and Standards

There is much debate about what should be the core competencies of leadership education. How one defines leadership, the theoretical frames chosen, and the unique learning histories of students all combine to make the articulation of leadership learning complex. Outcomes for leadership are often classified as knowledge outcomes, skills outcomes, attitudes and values outcomes, and behavioral outcomes (Driscoll & Wood, 2007). Several collaborative efforts have been made to articulate appropriate leadership-related learning outcomes for college students.

The International Leadership Association crafted a document called *Guiding Questions: Guidelines for Leadership Education Programs* that seeks to create frameworks to articulate both the essential nature and distinctiveness of individual leadership programs (ILA, 2009). The *Guidelines* are intended to assist anyone who wishes to develop, reorganize, or evaluate a leadership education program, and consist of five sections of questions that are thought to be essential for curriculum development, instructional effectiveness, and quality enhancement through assessment. These five sections are context, conceptual framework, content, teaching and learning, and outcomes and assessment (ILA, 2009). In the leadership content section, questions address the plurality of theories, definitions, philosophical and historical approaches, and disciplines that leadership educators have to choose from, but do not suggest a preferred set of leadership learning outcomes.

The *Standards for Student Leadership Programs* (SLPs) developed by Council for the Advancement of Standards in Higher Education attempt to codify the core competencies of leadership education (CAS, 2012). The CAS (2012) SLPs state that leadership programs "must advance student competencies in the categories of a) foundations of leadership, b) personal development, c) interpersonal development, and d) the development of groups, organizations, and systems" (p. 369). Table 1.1 depicts these competencies.

Other documents address leadership as one competency among many others. The RAND Corporation (2012) issued a report *Teaching and Learning 21st Century Skills: Lessons from the Learning Sciences*, which articulates leadership and collaboration as one of seven key skill sets for 21st century success (others include critical thinking and problem solving; agility and adaptability; accessing and analyzing information; effective oral and written communication; curiosity and imagination; and initiative and entrepreneurialism). The report encourages innovative pedagogies that emphasize the importance of creativity, problem solving, or applying knowledge to different contexts (Saavedra & Opfera, 2012). Similarly, the Association of American Colleges and Universities (AAC&U) initiative on *Liberal Education and America's Promise* (LEAP) enumerates 10 essential learning outcomes for student success (Rhodes, 2010). Though leadership is not explicitly listed, dimensions of leadership are nested in each of the 10 outcomes. Recently, Seemiller (2013) painstakingly mapped leadership competencies and models onto 522 unique degree program requirements as accredited by 97 different agencies, thus enabling educators to connect leadership development to a vast array of disciplines, learning goals, and curricula.

One further initiative to shape the core content of leadership learning is the Association of Leadership Educators (ALE) *National Leadership Education Research Agenda* (Andenoro et al., 2013). This document has the stated goals of defining research priorities that can guide applied scholarship contributing to the development of future leaders and managers through higher education, and providing key elements that further define leadership education as a discipline. The document articulates priorities in seven research areas, but does not go far enough in interrogating the underlying assumptions and unstated privileges embedded in the work of leadership education (Haber-Curran & Owen, 2013).

So how does a leadership educator select from the numerous competencies, standards, and pedagogical approaches in order to craft a meaningful learning experience for student leaders? The answer lies in educators themselves being willing to become lifelong learners and critical curators of leadership research, knowledge, and pedagogy.

New Directions for Student Leadership • DOI: 10.1002/yd

Leadership Educators and Critical Consciousness

Leadership educators, especially those in educational settings, are often "distracted by other responsibilities and isolated from others from whom they could learn about learning" (ACPA/NASPA, 1997, p. 1). Thus, well-intentioned individuals may fail to become skilled in the development of engaged pedagogy, integrative learning experiences, and intentional learning communities. There is a need for leadership practitioners to adopt the mantle of "educator," which requires intentional socialization to new knowledge, skills, and habits. Adopting an educator role requires more than just a shift in mindset—it also requires ongoing personal work. Leadership educators, usually unintentionally, are vulnerable to playing out their own privileges, preferences, and patterns on the students they encounter. Educators must work to identify and address how their own intersecting multiple identities, learning styles, and developmental experiences shape their work. Leadership practitioners who commit to the work of education in deep way have the potential to both transform themselves and provide transformative education to students (Owen, 2011).

Brookfield (2005) encourages educators to go beyond critical thinking, and to instead use critical theory to "extend democratic values and processes, to create a world in which a commitment to the common good is the foundation of well-being and development" (p. 32). To Brookfield, becoming a critically conscious educator involves helping learners challenge the beliefs and structures that serve only the interests of the few and instead learn to awaken and act on human agency. These directives are not far from relational, ethical, and socially responsible approaches to leadership popularly taught to students today (Burns, 1978; Higher Education Research Institute [HERI], 1996; Komives, Lucas, & McMahon, 2013). It stands to reason that leadership educators must interrogate their own biases, beliefs, and practices if they are to develop critical consciousness. Table 1.2 offers some reflection questions for growing in each of Brookfield's (2005) key learning tasks of critical theory.

Conclusion

If leadership educators are to transform the hearts and minds of leadership learners, they must first undertake their own journey of self-discovery and critical self-reflection. Paolo Freire (1970) states, "Knowledge emerges only through invention and re-invention, through the restless, impatient, continuing, hopeful inquiry human beings pursue in the world, with the world, and with each other" (p. 72). The chapters that follow in this volume invite readers to construct a coherent philosophy of effective and evidence-based leadership learning, which may involve deconstructing or dismantling certain assumptions about the nature of leadership learning along the way.

Table 1.2   Questions to Develop Critically Conscious Leadership Educators

The Learning Tasks of Critical Theory	Questions to Develop Critically Conscious Leadership Educators
Challenging ideology	How/where are leadership educators learning forms of reasoning and action that challenge social, cultural, and political ideologies? How are we modeling these processes for students?
Contesting hegemony	How are leadership educators learning about hegemony (according to Brookfield [2005])—"the process whereby people learn to embrace ideas, practices, and institutions that actually work against their own best interests" (p. 31)—and their own complicity in its continued existence? How might leadership itself intentionally or unintentionally support hegemonic processes?
Unmasking power	How are leadership educators learning to examine issues of power in their lives and communities? Where are leadership educators spending their privilege (Gorski, 2012) to create more equitable conditions for students and communities?
Overcoming alienation	How are leadership educators developing connectedness to others (as individuals, groups, and communities) and using these networks to draw on the power of the collective? How are we modeling these practices for students?
Learning liberation	To what extent do leadership educators challenge notions of groupthink or the dominance of the collective? Where do leadership learners experience individualized learning and support so that they can foster "rebellious subjectivity"? (Brookfield, 2005)
Reclaiming reason	To what extent do leadership educators inculcate the values of civil society in students (according to Brookfield [2005] "the relationships, associations, and institutions not directly under state control within which people for relationships and develop identities" [p. 31])?
Learning democracy	What are the links between leadership education and democratic values? How are students learning to practice democracy while embracing its many contradictions and tensions?
Teaching criticality	What does it mean to teach leadership from a critical perspective? How might leadership educators embrace deliberative dialogue and the collective creation of knowledge? What is the role of resistance in leadership education and development?

Source: Adapted from Brookfield (2005).

References

American College Personnel Association and National Association of Student Personnel Administrators (ACPA/NASPA). (1997). *Principles of good practice for student affairs.* Retrieved from http://acpa.nche.edu/pgp/principle.htm

Andenoro, A. C., Allen, S. J., Haber-Curran, P., Jenkins, D. M., Sowcik, M., Dugan, J. P., & Osteen, L. (2013). *National Leadership Education research agenda 2013–2018: Providing strategic direction for the field of leadership education.* Retrieved from http://leadershipeducators.org/ResearchAgenda

Anderson, L. W., & Krathwohl, D. R. (Eds.). (2001). *A taxonomy for learning, teaching, and assessing: A revision of Bloom's taxonomy of educational objectives.* Boston, MA: Allyn and Bacon.

Avolio, B. (2005). *Leadership development in balance.* Mahwah, NJ: Lawrence Erlbaum Associates.

Bass, B. M. (1990). *Bass & Stogdill's handbook of leadership: Theory, research, and managerial applications* (3rd ed.). New York, NY: Free Press.

Bloom, B. S. (1956). *Taxonomy of educational objectives, handbook I: The cognitive domain.* New York, NY: David McKay.

Bowen, J. A. (2012). *Teaching naked: How moving technology out of your college classroom will improve student learning.* San Francisco, CA: Jossey-Bass.

Brookfield, S. D. (2005). *The power of critical theory.* San Francisco, CA: Jossey-Bass.

Burns, J. M. (1978). *Leadership.* New York, NY: Harper & Row.

Council for the Advancement of Standards in Higher Education (CAS). (2012). *CAS professional standards for higher education* (8th ed.). Washington, DC: Author.

Daloz Parks, S. (2005). *Leadership can be taught.* Boston, MA: Harvard Business School Press.

Day, D. V., Harrison, M. M., & Halpin, S. M. (2009). *An integrative approach to leader development: Connecting adult development, identity, and expertise.* New York, NY: Routledge.

Driscoll, A., & Wood, S. (2007). *Developing outcomes-based assessment for learner-centered education.* Sterling, VA: Stylus.

Dugan, J. P., Bohle, C. W., Woelker, L. R., & Cooney, M. A. (2014). The role of social perspective-taking in developing students' leadership capacities. *Journal of Student Affairs Research and Practice, 51*(1), 1–15.

Dugan, J. P., Kodama, C., Correia, B., & Associates. (2013). *Multi-institutional study of leadership insight report: Leadership program delivery.* College Park, MD: National Clearinghouse for Leadership Programs.

Fink, L. D. (2003). *Creating significant learning experiences: An integrated approach to designing college courses.* San Francisco, CA: Jossey-Bass.

Fink, L. D. (2013). *Creating significant learning experiences: An integrated approach to designing college courses* (2nd ed.). San Francisco, CA: Jossey-Bass.

Freire, P. (1970). *Pedagogy of the oppressed.* New York, NY: Continuum.

Goleman, D. (1995). *Emotional intelligence.* New York, NY: Bantam Books.

Gorski, P. (2012). Equity and social justice from the inside out: Ten commitments for intercultural educators. In N. Palaiologou & G. Dietz (Eds.), *Mapping the broad field of multicultural and intercultural education worldwide: Toward the development of a new citizen* (pp. 388–401). Newcastle, UK: Cambridge Scholars Publishing.

Haber-Curran, P., & Owen, J. E. (2013). Engaging the whole student: Student affairs educators and the National Leadership Education Research Agenda. *Journal of Leadership Education, 12*(3), 38–50.

Higher Education Research Institute (HERI). (1996). *A social change model of leadership development.* College Park, MD: National Clearinghouse for Leadership Programs.

International Leadership Association (ILA). (2009). *Guiding questions: Guidelines for leadership education programs.* Retrieved from http://www.ila-net.org/communities/LC/GuidingQuestionsFinal.pdf

Jenkins, D. (2012, winter). Exploring signature pedagogies in undergraduate leadership education. *Journal of Leadership Education, 11*(1), 1–27.

Komives, S. R., Lucas, N., & McMahon, T. R. (2013). *Exploring leadership: For college students who want to make a difference* (3rd ed.). San Francisco, CA: Jossey-Bass.

Nelson, C. E. (2010). Dysfunctional illusions of rigor: Lessons from the scholarship of teaching and learning. In L. B. Nilson & J. E. Miller (Eds.), *To improve the academy: Resources for faculty, instructional, and organizational development* (Vol. 28, pp. 177–196). San Francisco, CA: Jossey-Bass.

Northouse, P. (2012). *Leadership: Theory and practice* (6th ed.). Thousand Oaks, CA: Sage.

Owen, J. E. (2011). Considerations of student learning in leadership. In S. R. Komives, J. P. Dugan, J. E. Owen, C. Slack, & W. Wagner, (Eds.), *The handbook for student leadership development* (2nd ed., pp. 109–133). San Francisco, CA: Jossey-Bass.

Preskill, S., & Brookfield, S. D. (2009). *Learning as a way of leading: Lessons from the struggle for social justice.* San Francisco, CA: Jossey-Bass.

RAND Corporation. (2012). *RAND Corporation 2012 Annual Report: Who are you listening to?* Retrieved from http://www.rand.org/pubs/corporate_pubs/CP1-2012.html

Rhodes, T. L. (2010). *Assessing outcomes and improving achievement: Tips and tools for using rubrics.* Washington, DC: Association of American Colleges & Universities.

Roberts, D. C. (2007). *Deeper learning in leadership.* San Francisco, CA: Jossey-Bass.

Saavedra, A. R., & Opfera, V. D. (2012). *Teaching and learning 21st century skills: Lessons from the learning sciences.* Washington, DC: RAND Corporation.

Seemiller, C. (2013). *The student leadership competencies guidebook: Designing intentional leadership learning and development.* San Francisco, CA: Jossey-Bass.

Shankman, M. L., Allen, S. J., & Haber-Curran, P. (in press). *Emotionally intelligent leadership: A guide for students* (2nd ed.). San Francisco, CA: Jossey-Bass.

Vaill, P. B. (1998). *Spirited leading and learning: Process wisdom for a new age.* San Francisco, CA: Jossey-Bass.

JULIE E. OWEN *is an associate professor of leadership and integrative studies and executive director of Social Action & Integrative Learning (SAIL) in New Century College at George Mason University.*

2

Cognitive elements of transformational learning, particularly metacognition and critical self-reflection, are discussed as essential considerations for leadership development in the 21st century. The importance of developmentally sequencing leadership-learning experiences and addressing evolving complexities of leadership identity are also explored.

Building Critical Capacities for Leadership Learning

Mark Anthony Torrez, Melissa L. Rocco

Thriving in this complex, interconnected, and diverse world requires critical thinking, adaptive leadership, and global perspectives that enable cross-border collaboration across differences of ideology and culture. While research in the field of leadership studies indicates modern notions of leadership as collaborative and process based (see Komives, Lucas, & McMahon, 2013; Rost, 1993; Yukl, 2006), most leadership development programs across schools and workplaces often fail to examine leadership as more than a static outcome or a singular skill (Day & Harrison, 2007; Lord & Hall, 2005).

The most progressive rhetoric surrounding 21st-century leadership calls for both the capacity to navigate complex systems and the resilience to persist through difficult barriers. This literature urges for integrated models of leadership that consider cognitive, psychosocial, and spiritual dimensions of human development in conjunction with—and at the core of—leader and leadership development processes (Bordas, 2007; Day, Harrison, & Halpin, 2009; Dugan, Bohle, Woelker, & Cooney, 2014; Dugan, Kodama, & Gebhardt, 2012; Guthrie, Bertrand Jones, Osteen, & Hu, 2013; Kezar, 2014). In order to thrive in this diverse and dynamic world, effective leadership requires less focus on tactile skills and outcomes, and instead centers learning as a critical capacity. In his taxonomy of significant learning, Fink (2013) calls this capacity *learning how to learn*.

Although the fundamental concept of learning is inherent to most human development theories and leadership models (Debebe, 2011; Kegan, 1994; Kolb, 1983; Preskill & Brookfield, 2009), few explicitly address this

New Directions for Student Leadership, no. 145, Spring 2015 © 2015 Wiley Periodicals, Inc., A Wiley Company
Published online in Wiley Online Library (wileyonlinelibrary.com) • DOI: 10.1002/yd.20121

cognitive process (Day et al., 2009; Owen, 2011; Roberts, 2007), which has resulted in a significant disconnect between the body of literature that examines student learning and the literature that examines student leadership development. Yet, if the nature of the 21st century compels leaders to exhibit capacities for mental flexibility, resilience, and learning, attention must be given to the cognitive processes that make student leadership development possible. This chapter centers learning as the critical capacity for transformation and advocates a stronger consideration of the individual learning process that undergirds student leadership development.

Transformational Learning in Higher Education

Although learning is an age-old and universal idea, it is a concept that has been translated, contextualized, and tailored to hold a variety of definitions. Over centuries, this process of cultural and pedagogical variation has subtly, but surely, directed societal attention to the outcomes of learning such as skill development and career readiness, rather than the process in and of itself. For purposes of this discussion, learning is perceived not simply as informative or additive in nature, such as the activity or process of acquiring knowledge or skill; rather, learning is understood as more complex and transformational. While the utilization of a specific definition certainly creates limitations to exploring the philosophical complexity of learning, it enables redirecting discussion to the cognitive processes that are least understood yet elemental to the concept itself.

Over the past 80 years, several foundational documents have revolutionized higher education's approach to learning and the manner in which students are engaged, highlighting the critical importance of holistic learning that permeates both curricular and cocurricular environments (ACPA/NASPA, 2004; American College Personnel Association [ACPA], 1994; American Council on Education [ACE], 1937, 1949; Joint Task Force on Student Learning, 1998; Association of American Colleges and Universities [AAC&U], 2005). Furthermore, when focusing on the field of student affairs, most of the prominent literature underlines a consensus that identity formation is an essential component to student learning (Chickering & Reisser, 1993; Joint Task Force on Student Learning, 1998), impacting the way students "see themselves contributing to and participating in the world in which they live" (ACPA/NASPA, 2004, p. 9). This integration of student learning and development is characteristic of higher education and student affairs philosophy, and is increasingly relevant to leadership education.

Unfortunately, disciplinary silos have created barriers to enacting these espoused values and philosophy. In response, higher education leaders called publicly for more integrative approaches to student learning and development in the document *Learning Reconsidered: A Campus-Wide Focus on the Student Experience* (ACPA/NASPA, 2004):

Although there was once an element of utility in separating these theories, distinctions between learning and development are no longer helpful and may be destructive (Baxter Magolda, 1999). Transformative learning provides a unified theory of learning and development that transcends outmoded ideas about learning and questions the structure of most institutions of higher education. (p. 11)

The document embraced Mezirow's (1991, 2000) theory of *transformational learning* in its "reconsideration" of the purpose of higher education as transformative. Mezirow's (1991) theory articulates a weaving of student development and student learning—the two as integrally connected and bolstering of one another. More complex than simple knowledge or skill attainment, Mezirow (2000) described transformational learning as the process by which individuals liberate themselves from "reified forms of thought that are no longer dependable" (p. 27), given evolving contexts and the dynamic nature of the knowledge, situations, and problems individuals are confronted with therein.

Transformational learning can be related to Kolb's (1983) work on experiential learning in that it identifies a cyclical pattern of knowledge cultivation: encountering a concrete experience, engaging in reflection and meaning making, and then integrating knowledge gained as insight for future experiences. Mezirow (2000) similarly articulated the transformational learning process as encountering a dilemma, making meaning of the dilemma through intentional reflection, and then achieving transformative insight that enables the individual to engage in deeper, more complex forms of learning. The third component of the transformational learning process—achieving transformative insight—differentiates the concept from informative and experiential learning models in that it articulates cognitive evolution as both a process and outcome of the learning cycle. This type of learning does not simply provide new insight for future experiences but actually transforms the individual into a new, more complex way of knowing and being. The concept aligns closely with Kegan's (1994) Orders of Consciousness Model, which proposes a lifespan theory of cognitive development in which individuals undergo transformation in cognitive complexity as they move through "cognitive thresholds."

The theory of transformational learning (Mezirow, 1991, 2000) is highly applicable to most theories of student development and leadership development, particularly when considering identity-based theories of student leadership development (e.g., Leadership Identity Development [LID] model). In order to better understand and apply transformational learning to student leadership development, the following sections dissect and build on critical elements of the transformational learning process: metacognition and critical self-reflection, leadership identity development, and developmental sequencing.

NEW DIRECTIONS FOR STUDENT LEADERSHIP • DOI: 10.1002/yd

Metacognition and Critical Self-Reflection

When examining key student learning and development theories, such as Kegan's (1994) Orders of Consciousness Model and Mezirow's (2000) Transformative Learning Process, a pattern emerges: individuals evolve from simple to more complex forms of knowing, being, and doing. Research on leadership development from both within and outside of formal educational systems such as high school or college supports a similar theme of progression. As one develops cognitively and psychosocially, one's understanding and practice of leadership changes and becomes more complex (Avolio & Hannah, 2008; Komives, Longerbeam, Mainella, Osteen, & Owen, 2009; Komives, Longerbeam, Owen, Mainella, & Osteen, 2006; Komives, Owen, Longerbeam, Mainella, & Osteen, 2005; Ligon, Hunter, & Mumford, 2008; Lord & Hall, 2005).

Less commonly understood is the phenomenon of *metacognition*, or "the process of thinking about our thinking," that serves as the primary mechanism by which transformational learning and development are facilitated. If cognition is the overarching process by which an individual engages in mental tasks, such as acquiring new knowledge, then metacognition is the act of monitoring the cognitive process itself (Day et al., 2009). An individual engaging in the metacognitive process acknowledges what he or she is thinking, examines and questions his or her thoughts and thought processes, and then integrates previous understanding with new knowledge and experiences to develop new perspectives. These processes include critical self-reflection and the developmental sequencing of learning.

    Critical Self-Reflection.   Reflection is a core element of the metacognitive process and a fundamental practice of nearly all learning and development models. However, much like learning, the idea and meaning of reflection has become confounded for many educators largely because of a lack of strong pedagogical foundation. Even within service learning—a discipline grounded in the reflective nature of experiential learning—educators struggle to define and employ reflection (Jacoby & Associates, 1996). In an effort to clarify meaning and enhance practicality, educators leverage the specific concept of *critical self-reflection* as the keystone to metacognition, transformational learning, and powerful student leadership development.

Whereas the traditional form of reflection generically refers to the mental acknowledgement of feelings, thoughts, attitudes, and beliefs toward content or experience, critical self-reflection "involves a critique of the presuppositions on which our beliefs have been built" (Mezirow, 1990, p. 1). For example, consider that a college student body president recently conducted a series of interviews for upcoming cabinet transitions. After engaging in reflection, she ranked the candidates she felt were strongest in the interview process—a mental task that is pseudo-consciously guided by her understanding of leadership. However, if she were to engage in critical self-reflection, she would have paused to more directly consider her perspectives on leadership, where they might have originated, and how they may result in biased decision making. She may have then become aware that her view of leadership privileged those who were decisive and self-confident and disadvantaged those who were facilitative and group centered. Critical self-reflection is the process by which individuals acknowledge the very lens through which they see the world, problematize situations, and sort and organize information for situational action (Day et al., 2009; Mezirow, 1990).

Critical self-reflection is often instigated by a *disorienting dilemma* (Mezirow, 1990). Disorienting dilemmas come in many forms and are unique to the individual. Examples might include a powerful book, the death of a family member, a compelling lecture or group discussion, traveling abroad, being assigned new responsibilities at work, and/or meeting someone from a different cultural background. Regardless of the specific context, disorienting dilemmas trigger critical self-reflection because they introduce content or experiences that do not fit within previously held frames of reference or meaning perspectives. The dissonance experienced by an individual instigates an acknowledgement of and reflection upon one's presuppositions and often results in cognitive transformation. Therefore, critical self-reflection is the mechanism by which Mezirow's (2000) transformational learning process functions: the process by which one confronts and evolves inherent meaning-making structures.

In considering the purpose and benefit of critical self-reflection, it is important to recognize that the lifespan process of learning and cognitive development can result in various forms of distortion within an individual's frames of reference or meaning perspectives. According to Mezirow (1990), "Meaning perspectives are transformed through a critically reflective assessment of epistemic, sociocultural, and psychic distortions acquired through the process of introjection, the uncritical acceptance of another's values" (p. 14). Epistemic distortions impact the ways in which individuals come to understand and view the nature of knowledge; sociocultural distortion refers to "taking for granted belief systems that refer to power and social relationships" (Mezirow, 1990, p. 15); and psychic distortions are deeply held frames of reference that actually serve to create anxiety and inhibit personal action (Mezirow, 1990). By engaging in critical self-reflection, individuals confront meaning and perspective distortions resultant from the passive and uncritical adoption of values. In this sense, critical self-reflection is less concerned with the actual behavior or decision and more interested in uncovering or deconstructing the "why" or reasoning for the behavior or decision.

Applications to Leadership.   Within the realm of student leadership development, the metacognitive process of critical self-reflection is pivotal in facilitating the confrontation of previously held assumptions, or distortions, regarding definitions and values associated with leadership. Research demonstrates that one's meaning perspectives and assumptions can either bolster or diminish leadership motivation, self-efficacy, identity, and capacity—and their interplay inevitably influences trajectories for enacted leader behavior (Komives et al., 2005, 2006, 2009). In considering one of the most widely used models of college student leadership, the social change model of leadership development (SCM) (Higher Education Research Institute [HERI], 1996), it is important to recognize how critical self-reflection serves as a catalyst for development within the Individual Values Domain. If one is unable to identify and confront one's own presuppositions, it is impossible to achieve growth within the values of this domain—consciousness of self, congruence, and commitment—all of which have a tremendous impact on a leader's ability to be effective in groups and create positive social change. Therefore, by placing increased emphasis on the metacognitive process of critical self-reflection, educators equip individuals with tremendous mental tools that can be used to dismantle barriers to leadership identity, self-efficacy, motivation, capacity, and behavior, thereby forging stronger pathways for exponential leader and leadership development.

Leadership Identity Development and Transformative Learning

Within the context of college student leadership development, perspective transformation is key to the work of educators. Mezirow (1990) defines perspective transformation as:

> the process of becoming critically aware of how and why our presuppositions have come to constrain the way we perceive, understand, and feel about our world; of reformulating these assumptions to permit a more inclusive, discriminating, permeable, and integrative perspective; and of making decisions or otherwise acting upon these new understandings. (p. 14)

An example of perspective transformation as applied to leadership development can be found in the scholarship on LID (Komives et al., 2005, 2006, 2009). This grounded theory study published in 2005 helped uncover how individuals evolve in their understanding of leadership as they simultaneously develop other aspects of human identity. Using a life narrative methodology, participants shared aspects of their experience from their youth through to the time of their interviews. From their findings, the research team created the LID model, a lifespan development model similar in process to transformative learning. The LID model highlights a gradual process whereby individuals move from (a) understanding leadership as external to the self and position-based, through (b) identifying the self as leader, into (c) an understanding of multiple perspectives and group leadership, and eventually toward (d) a complex and advanced form of leadership characterized by a sense of self-efficacy that enables the individual to be interdependent with others in a relational leadership process (see Table 2.1). Essentially, individuals engage in a perspective transformation through the metacognitive process in order to advance through the LID stages. First, an individual's view of self and others in the context of leadership changes as he or she moves through the six stages of the LID model. Those in the earliest stages (1 and 2) are *dependent* on others who are in leadership roles. In stage 3, individuals begin to identify themselves either *independent* of others when they are "the leader," or *dependent* on others when they are not in a positional leadership role and are a "follower." In the later LID stages (4, 5, and 6), individuals see their involvement in leadership as *interdependent* with others, recognizing their personal contributions to leadership while also incorporating and valuing the leadership of others in a collaborative process. They view leadership also as nonpositional and as a process.

There are similarities to both Mezirow's (1991) theory of Transformational Learning and Kegan's (1994) Orders of Consciousness in the way individuals move through the LID model: individuals incorporate knowledge and perspectives from previous stages into each subsequent stage and may cycle back through previous stages. Specifically with the LID model, individuals may utilize leadership approaches from stages they have already surpassed, but they will maintain their leadership identity in the highest stage achieved (Komives et al., 2005, 2006, 2009). For example, a college student may successfully hold a formal leadership position in a student organization long after he or she has already come to know and understand leadership as something that anyone can contribute to with or without a title.

Developmental Sequencing

If critical self-reflection is key to leadership learning and development, then how do educators go about creating opportunities for diverse students to engage in this process? While leadership approaches have evolved to become more collaborative and relational, many leadership development programs are still focused on one-size-fits-all content and skill-based training rather than transformational learning for advancing the human development process (Day & Harrison, 2007; Day et al., 2009; Lord & Hall, 2005). Helping students to develop understanding of, capacity for, and efficacy around modern, complex approaches to leadership requires intentional, developmentally appropriate curriculum design and implementation. It is essential that knowledge of cognitive development and transformational learning are used to inform the practice of creating leadership development programs. This is true even for leadership skill building, which can be taught pro forma, or can be developmentally sequenced based on the LID stage, multiple identities, and needs of the learner. For example, one of the values of the SCM (HERI, 1996) is handling controversy with civility. This skill might be developed through first learning active listing skills, learning how to frame an issue from another's perspective, how to share one's own point of view in a nondefensive manner, and how to perception check calmly with others inviting questions and comments on one's own views.

Table 2.1 Leadership Identity Development Model

Stages →	1 Awareness		2 Exploration/Engagement		3 Leader Identified	
Key categories		*Transition*		*Transition*	*Emerging*	*Immersion*
Stage descriptions	• Recognizing that leadership is happening around you • Getting exposure to involvements		• Intentional involvements (sports, religious institutions, service, scouts, dance, SGA) • Experiencing groups for the first time • Taking on responsibilities		• Trying on new roles • Identifying skills needed • Taking on individual responsibility • Individual accomplishments important	• Getting things done • Managing others • Practicing different approaches/styles *Leadership seen largely as positional roles held by self or others; leaders do leadership*
Broadening view of leadership	"Other people are leaders; leaders are out there somewhere"	"I am not a leader"	"I want to be involved"	"I want to do more"	"A leader gets things done"	"I am the leader and others follow me" or "I am a follower looking to the leader for direction"
Developing self	• Becomes aware of national leaders and authority figures (e.g., the principal)	• Want to make friends	• Develop personal skills • Identify personal strengths/weaknesses • Prepare for leadership • Build self-confidence	• Recognize personal leadership potential • Motivation to change something	• Positional leadership roles or group member roles • Narrow down to meaningful experiences (e.g., sports, clubs, yearbook, scouts, class projects)	• Models others • Leader struggles with delegation • Moves in and out of leadership roles and member roles but still believes the leader is in charge • Appreciates individual recognition

Group influences	• Uninvolved or "inactive" follower	• Want to get involved	• "Active" follower or member • Engage in diverse contexts (e.g., sports, clubs, class projects) • Affirmation of adults • Attributions (others see me as a leader)	Narrow interests	• Leader has to get things done • Group has a job to do; organize to get tasks done	• Involve members to get the job done • Stick with a primary group as an identity base; explore other groups
Developmental influences	Affirmation by adults (parents, teachers, coaches, scout leaders, religious elders)	• Observation/ watching • Recognition • Adult sponsors	• Role models • Older peers as sponsors • Adult sponsors • Assume positional roles • Reflection/ retreat		Take on responsibilities	• Model older peers and adults • Observe older peers • Adults as mentors, guides, coaches
Changing view of self with others	Dependent				Dependent Independent	

(Continued)

Table 2.1 Continued

The KEY	4 Leadership Differentiated			5 Generativity		6 Integration/Synthesis
	Emerging	*Immersion*	*Transition*	*Generativity*	*Transition*	*Integration/ Synthesis*
Transition						
• Shifting order of consciousness • Take on more complex leadership challenges	• Joining with others in shared tasks/goals from positional or nonpositional group roles • Need to learn group skills *New belief that leadership can come from anywhere in the group (nonpositional)*	• Seeks to facilitate a good group process whether in positional or nonpositional leader role • Commitment to community of the group *Awareness that leadership is a group process*		• Active commitment to a personal passion • Accepting responsibility for the development of others • Promotes team learning • Responsible for sustaining organizations		• Continued self-development and lifelong learning • Striving for congruence and internal confidence
"Holding a position does not mean I am a leader"	"I need to lead in a participatory way and I can contribute to leadership from anywhere in the organization"; "I can be a leader without a title"; "I am a leader even if I am not the leader"	"Leadership is happening everywhere; leadership is a process; we are doing leadership together; we are all responsible"	"Who's coming after me?"	"I am responsible as a member of my communities to facilitate the development of others as leaders and enrich the life of our groups"	"I need to be true to myself in all situations and open to grow"	"I know I am able to work effectively with others to accomplish change from any place in the organization"; "I am a leader"

			Interdependent			
• Recognition that I cannot do it all myself • Learn to value the importance/talent of others • Meaningfully engage with others • Look to group resources • Older peers as sponsors and mentors • Adults as mentors and meaning makers • Learning about leadership	• Learn to trust and value others and their involvement • Openness to other perspectives • Develop comfort leading as an active member • Practices being engaged member • Values servant leadership • Let go control • Seeing the collective whole; the big picture • Learn group and team skills • Practicing leadership in ongoing peer relationships	• Learn about personal influence • Effective in both positional and nonpositional roles • Value teams • Value connectedness to others • Learns how system works • Responds to meaning makers (student affairs staff, key faculty, same-age peer mentors)	• Focus on passion, vision, and commitments • Want to serve society • Value process • Seek fit with organization vision • Begins coaching others	• Sponsor and develop others • Transforming leadership • Concern for leadership pipeline • Concerned with sustainability of ideas • Sustaining the organization • Ensuring continuity in areas of passion/focus • Responds to meaning makers (student affairs staff, same-age peer mentors)	• Openness to ideas • Learning from others • Anticipating transition to new roles • Shared learning • Reflection/retreat	• Sees leadership as a lifelong developmental process • Want to leave things better • Am trustworthy and value that I have credibility • Recognition of role modeling to others • Sees organizational complexity across contexts • Can imagine how to engage with different organizations • Recycle when context changes or is uncertain (contextual uncertainty); enables continual recycling through leadership stages

Source: Originally published as: Komives, S. R., Longerbeam, S. D., Owen, J. E., Mainella, F. C., & Osteen, L. (2006). A leadership identity development model: Applications from a grounded theory. *Journal of College Student Development, 47*, 401–418. Used with permission.

Developmental sequencing is the pedagogical method of scaffolding learning opportunities to provide the appropriate amount of challenge that maximizes gains and minimizes losses for a student at a particular level of development. Proper developmental sequencing ultimately promotes positive growth along a particular developmental trajectory (Day et al., 2009). In the case of leadership learning, the LID model (Komives et al., 2005, 2006, 2009) becomes a powerful guide for developmental sequencing. The ideal developmental trajectory would be toward understanding leadership as relational, collaborative, and process focused. An integration of the concepts of transformational learning, cognitive development, and developmental sequencing would support that educators creating leadership development experiences should construct and deliver curriculum in a way that both challenges a student's current thoughts about leadership and supports the student through the often provocative nature of critical self-reflection. Through the metacognitive process, students are engaged in transformational learning that promotes positive development toward a more advanced leadership identity. From a practical standpoint, it is important to recognize that each individual involved in a leadership program, course, or experience may enter at varying stages in his or her human development. Thus, what may promote positive leadership development in one person may be too challenging or not challenging enough to promote development in others. Educators must keep the need for individuation in mind as they develop and deliver leadership curriculum, which is why developmental sequencing is of utmost importance.

As discussed throughout this chapter, metacognition and critical self-reflection are important considerations for leadership educators in that they activate the paradigmatic shifts and transformation espoused as outcomes of both leadership and liberal arts education. For example, consider a group of first-year student leaders who volunteer at a homeless shelter as a component of their orientation experience. Although each member of the group engages in similar volunteering, the meaning derived from the experience, and perhaps their behavior within the experience, are likely differentiated based on their perspectives or frames of reference crafted prior to coming to college. In fact, research indicates that precollege exposures are one of the most significant factors in college student leadership trajectories (Dugan & Komives, 2010). However, these experiential resources remain largely untapped because educators struggle to leverage critical self-reflection as a tool to assist students in the process of mentally accessing those presuppositions. For the first-year volunteers, it may be helpful to structure intentional reflection exercises that do not simply gauge surface-level satisfaction or learning, but more importantly invite them to confront their understanding of, motivations for, and underlying perspectives on leadership and volunteering.

This could include helping a student who experienced discomfort and fear during the volunteer experience deconstruct the ways in which classist stereotypes craft public perceptions of homelessness and better recognize how power, privilege, and oppression influenced their leader behavior in that situation—as well as how that insight may frame new understandings of leadership and affect how they interact across difference in the future. Therefore, by engaging students in critically self-reflective discourse on their meaning perspectives—most of which are developed during childhood and early adolescence—educators position young adults to deconstruct epistemic, sociocultural, and psychic distortions that may serve to inhibit or impede their college learning and leadership development.

Critical Reflection Questions.   Leadership educators may find it useful to guide critical reflection by asking compelling questions. Prompts for examining and challenging personal paradigms about leadership in diverse communities (e.g., after a service-learning experience) might include:

- What about engaging with this community was challenging for you?
- Who in this community did you learn something from today? What did they teach you?
- What did you assume about leadership in this community before today's experience?
- How did you see leadership happen in this community today? How does that differ from the assumptions you made about leadership in this community? How does that differ from how you viewed leadership generally prior to this experience?
- How do assumptions, biases, and stereotypes influence how we engage others in the process of leadership?
- Optional prompt, if developmentally appropriate: How do assumptions, biases, and stereotypes influence how *you* engage others in the process of leadership?

Prompts to promote transition from leader identified (LID stage 3) views to leadership differentiated (LID stage 4) views (e.g., following a leadership workshop or retreat) might include:

- Talk about the unique skills and talents that each of your peers brought to this experience today.
- What surprised you about the way people contributed to this experience? How does that differ from what you expected?
- In what ways did you see people help the group function better as a team?
- How did you see those without a title show leadership in this experience?
- Were there times when you shared your opinion or made the decision for the group when you really could have or should have let someone else take the lead? Discuss further.

- Where else in your life have you seen people lead without a title or formal position?
- What are three things you can do to empower others in your next group leadership experience?
- What assumptions did you make about who can lead and how leadership happens before this experience? What personal experiences informed those assumptions?
- How has your view of leadership changed after this experience?

Final Thoughts

The purpose of this chapter was to explore the cognitive processes that are inherent to transformational learning and leadership development. As educators, we are equally compelled to critically examine the paradigms, presuppositions, and perspectives from which we structure and facilitate leadership development. Too often the focus of leadership programs remains on specific leadership behaviors and the attempt to change them at the surface level. Yet, evidence demonstrates that this is rarely effective in facilitating lasting leadership development. This remains one of the great ironies of leadership education: leadership is considered an outcome when in fact it should be viewed, treated, and practiced as a continual learning process, influenced by corresponding trajectories in human development. As discussed throughout this chapter, cognitive frameworks that guide behavior demand more attention and consideration in leadership education. If the goal is to truly create more socially responsible leaders in action, not just in theory, leadership educators must commit to understanding and confronting the underlying cognitive learning processes that move students from simple to more complex frames of mind. The centering of learning as a critical capacity in leadership development is an important step in better preparing students for the complex leadership challenges of the 21st century.

References

American College Personnel Association (ACPA). (1994). *The student learning imperative: Implications for student affairs.* Washington, DC: Author.

American College Personnel Association/National Association of Student Personnel Administrators (ACPA/NASPA). (2004). *Learning reconsidered: A campus-wide focus on the student experience.* Washington, DC: Author.

American Council on Education (ACE). (1937). *The student personnel point of view: A report of a conference on the philosophy and development of student personnel work in colleges and universities* (American Council on Education Studies Series 1, Vol. 1, No. 3). Washington, DC: Author.

American Council on Education (ACE). (1949). *The student personnel point of view* (rev. ed.). (American Council on Education Studies Series 6, Vol. 13, No. 13). Washington, DC: Author.

Association of American Colleges and Universities (AAC&U). (2005). *Liberal education and America's promise: Excellence for everyone as a nation goes to college.* Washington, DC: Author.

Avolio, B. J., & Hannah, S. T. (2008). Developmental readiness: Accelerating leader development. *Consulting Psychology Journal: Practice and Research, 60,* 331–347.

Bordas, J. (2007). *Salsa, soul, and spirit: Leadership for a multi-cultural age.* San Francisco, CA: Berrett-Koehler.

Chickering, A. W., & Reisser, L. (1993). *Education and identity* (2nd ed.). San Francisco, CA: Jossey-Bass.

Day, D. V., & Harrison, M. M. (2007). A multilevel, identity-based approach to leadership development. *Human Resource Management Review, 17,* 360–373.

Day, D. V., Harrison, M. M., & Halpin, S. M. (2009). *An integrative approach to leader development: Connecting adult development, identity, and expertise.* New York, NY: Routledge.

Debebe, G. (2011). Creating a safe environment for women's leadership transformation. *Journal of Management Education, 35,* 679–712.

Dugan, J. P., Bohle, C. W., Woelker, L. R., & Cooney, M. A. (2014). The role of social perspective-taking in developing students' leadership capacities. *Journal of Student Affairs Research and Practice, 51,* 1–15.

Dugan, J. P., Kodama, C. M., & Gebhardt, M. C. (2012). Race and leadership development among college students: The additive value of collective racial esteem. *Journal of Diversity in Higher Education, 5,* 174–189.

Dugan, J. P., & Komives, S. R. (2010). Influences on college students' capacity for socially responsible leadership. *Journal of College Student Development, 51,* 525–549.

Fink, L. D. (2013). *Creating significant learning experiences: An integrated approach to designing college courses* (2nd ed.). San Francisco, CA: Jossey-Bass.

Guthrie, K. L., Bertrand Jones, T., Osteen, L., & Hu, S. (2013). *Cultivating leader identity and capacity in students from diverse backgrounds* [ASHE Higher Education Report, 39(4)]. San Francisco, CA: Jossey-Bass.

Higher Education Research Institute (HERI). (1996). *A social change model of leadership development.* College Park, MD: National Clearinghouse for Leadership Programs.

Jacoby, B., & Associates. (1996). *Service-learning in higher education: Concepts and practices.* San Francisco, CA: Jossey-Bass.

Joint Task Force on Student Learning. (1998, June 2). *Powerful partnerships: A shared responsibility for student learning.* Retrieved from http://www.acpa.nche.edu/powerful -partnerships-shared-responsibility-learning

Kegan, R. (1994). *In over our heads: The mental demands of modern life.* Cambridge, MA: Harvard University Press.

Kezar, A. (2014). *How colleges change: Understanding, leading, and enacting change.* New York, NY: Routledge.

Kolb, D. (1983). *Experiential learning: Experience as the source of learning and development.* Englewood Cliffs, NJ: Prentice Hall.

Komives, S. R., Longerbeam, S., Mainella, F. C., Osteen, L., & Owen, J. E. (2009). Leadership identity development: Challenges in applying a developmental model. *Journal of Leadership Education, 8,* 11–47.

Komives, S. R., Longerbeam, S., Owen, J. E., Mainella, F. C., & Osteen, L. (2006). A leadership identity development model: Applications from a grounded theory. *Journal of College Student Development, 47,* 401–420.

Komives, S. R., Owen, J. E., Longerbeam, S., Mainella, F. C., & Osteen, L. (2005). Developing a leadership identity: A grounded theory. *Journal of College Student Development, 46,* 593–611.

Komives, S. R., Lucas, N., & McMahon, T. R. (2013). *Exploring leadership: For college students who want to make a difference* (3rd ed.). San Francisco, CA: Jossey-Bass.

Ligon, G. S., Hunter, S. T., & Mumford, M. D. (2008). Development of outstanding leadership: A life narrative approach. *The Leadership Quarterly, 19*, 312–334.

Lord, R. G., & Hall, R. J. (2005). Identity, deep structure, and the development of leadership skill. *Leadership Quarterly, 16*, 591–615.

Mezirow, J. (1990). How critical reflection triggers transformative learning. In J. Mezirow (Ed.), *Fostering critical reflection in adulthood* (pp. 1–20). San Francisco, CA: Jossey-Bass.

Mezirow, J. (1991). *Transformative dimensions in adult learning.* San Francisco, CA: Jossey-Bass.

Mezirow, J. (2000). *Learning as transformation: Critical perspectives on a theory in progress.* San Francisco, CA: Jossey-Bass.

Owen, J. E. (2011). Considerations of student learning in leadership. In S. R. Komives, J. P. Dugan, J. E. Owen, C. Slack, & W. Wagner (Eds.), *The handbook for student leadership development* (2nd ed., pp. 109–133). San Francisco, CA: Jossey-Bass.

Preskill, S., & Brookfield, S. D. (2009). *Learning as a way of leading: Lessons from the struggle for social justice.* San Francisco, CA: Jossey-Bass.

Roberts, D. C. (2007). *Deeper learning in leadership: Helping college students find the potential within.* San Francisco, CA: Jossey-Bass.

Rost, J. C. (1993). *Leadership for the twenty-first century.* Westport, CT: Praeger.

Yukl, G. A. (2006). *Leadership in organizations* (6th ed.). Upper Saddle River, NJ: Prentice Hall.

MARK ANTHONY TORREZ *is a doctoral student at Loyola University Chicago and project manager for the Multi-Institutional Study of Leadership.*

MELISSA L. ROCCO *is a doctoral student at the University of Maryland College Park and graduate coordinator and instructor for the Leadership Studies Program.*

NEW DIRECTIONS FOR STUDENT LEADERSHIP • DOI: 10.1002/yd

Leadership education that intentionally addresses critical, creative, and practical thinking enhances significant learning for students and deepens the leadership practices of educators. This chapter explores specific applications in the areas of graduate leadership education, action research, service immersion program, and advising conversations. Additionally, it presents a framework of pathways to social change and suggests how such a framework can be useful to students and leadership educators.

Navigating Leadership Complexity Through Critical, Creative, and Practical Thinking

Jennifer M. Pigza

The six elements of Fink's (2013) Taxonomy of Significant Learning present a relational and interactive framework both to design learning experiences as well as to analyze those that have already occurred. This chapter specifically focuses on the domain of application knowledge, and even more specifically the three types of thinking—critical, creative, and practical—and how they foster leadership development, innovation, and effectiveness.

Leadership for social change requires an awareness of the complexity of both the issues at hand and the process of change itself. A deep exploration of thinking serves three purposes: it allows leadership educators to be more wide-awake in the practice of leadership both with students and in other spheres of influence; it assists learners in noticing and navigating leadership complexity; and guides educators in crafting learning experiences that meet desired learning and development goals. In other words, this chapter aims to deepen teaching-facilitating skills, and in doing so engage the self-reflective processes of leadership educators.

After an introduction to Fink's (2013) critical, creative, and practical thinking and their usefulness in leadership education, the chapter presents a microscopic, macroscopic, and mirror perspective of their application. The microscopic view explores specific applications in the areas of graduate leadership education, action research, a service immersion program, and

New Directions for Student Leadership, no. 145, Spring 2015 © 2015 Wiley Periodicals, Inc., A Wiley Company
Published online in Wiley Online Library (wileyonlinelibrary.com) • DOI: 10.1002/yd.20122

advising conversations. The macrosopic view presents framework of pathways to social change, explores how triarchic thinking is necessary in each (i.e., critical thinking, creative thinking, and practical thinking), and suggests how such a framework can be useful to students and educators. The third presents a mirror to leadership educators and asks what is required of ourselves in our pursuit of leadership for social change.

Application Knowledge, Thinking, and Leadership Education

Fink's (2013) notion of "application learning" is categorized as critical, creative, and practical thinking, as well as managing complex projects and developing performance skills. Application learning is the process by which learners shift from acquisition of knowledge to developing the skills and capacities to do something new—and useful—with it. This type of learning can be intellectual (integration of new ideas), physical (embodiment practices), and social (development of group skills). For example, in an undergraduate leadership course, a student might learn about the differences between industrial and postindustrial models of leadership (Rost, 1993) and observe how these models are evident in daily leadership practices. The application of that knowledge occurs when a student attempts to operate differently in a leadership role, perhaps by being less hierarchical in her or his decision making.

While the main thrust of the scholarship of teaching and learning focuses on the notion of critical thinking, Fink (2013) invites educators to consider the merits of Sternberg's (1989) triarchic view of thinking which includes critical thinking, creative thinking, and practical thinking. By adopting this categorization, Fink creates opportunities for leadership educators to become more specific in our approaches, both in study and in practice. Table 3.1 links the three types of thinking, learning goals described by Fink, and how learning goals are often labeled within leadership education.

Table 3.1   Triarchic Thinking and Leadership Education

	Fink's (2013) Learning Goal	Learning Goals Within Leadership Education
Critical thinking	Fosters abilities to analyze, evaluate and critique; assess multiple interpretations; explain results; predict future outcomes	Leadership development
Creative thinking	Invites new ideas, questions, products, and perspectives; engages multiple forms of expression	Leadership innovation
Practical thinking	Develops problem-solving and decision-making capabilities; supports action-oriented choices	Leadership effectiveness

Triarchic thinking connected to leadership education is evident in the following example. Resident assistants on a campus recently galvanized a group of their peers to bring the unspoken challenges of low-income students on campus to consciousness. In preparation for their resident assistant position, the students had taken a leadership course framed in the social change model of leadership (Komives, Wagner, & Associates, 2009). They engaged in all three types of thinking in their exercise of leadership. First, *critical thinking*: Grounded in their knowledge of the social change model, the students evaluated the situation at the individual, group, and institutional levels. They named the problem of student poverty as they understood it and lived it. Second, *creative thinking*: The group developed a plan for a large-scale event promoted to students exclusively through social media and utilized grassroots organizing tactics to involve nearly two dozen faculty, staff, administrators, and trustees. Third, *practical thinking*: The students developed an effective strategy to invite the entire campus to a dialogue about student poverty. Through a world-café style event (Brown & Isaacs, 2005) for over 200 people, the group raised the profile of the issue of student poverty, created space for personal narrative sharing around the issue, and generated new ideas for supporting students.

In this example, the types of thinking of Fink's (2013) taxonomy of significant learning are applied post hoc, after the fact. The resident assistants were acting *after* their experience of the leadership course, and yet, their efforts are evidence of critical, creative, and practical thinking, of leadership development, innovation, and effectiveness. What would happen if these learning goals were intentionally named within the curriculum of that course? How might students' learning have deepened if they had a metaunderstanding of these learning goals? What might students learn about their exercise of leadership if given an opportunity for intentional reflection about their campus activism?

Leadership educators are well advised to be transparent with students about their learning goals and to integrate reflective questions that bridge theory-to-practice into planning and debriefing conversations. An integrative approach, while requiring greater intentionality for the leadership educator, serves to affirm and bring forward the complexity that students are already experiencing and enhances their learning.

Thinking and Leadership for Social Change

This section offers a detailed-level view of how application knowledge and triarchic thinking can be embedded in leadership education. Each example begins with a theoretical orientation, connects it to leadership for social change, and then dives in to specifics.

Graduate Leadership Education and Action Research for Social Change. Action research engages the researcher(s) with collaborative partners to create significant change in human systems. Three core principles frame all of action research: it is change oriented, cyclical, and participatory (Reason & Bradbury-Huang, 2006). The action research family includes many forms and methods, including human inquiry, action inquiry, action learning, action science, and participatory inquiry (Brooks & Watkins, 1994). In its many manifestations, action research maintains the assurances of qualitative research while also pushing the boundaries through a consideration of the whole-person role of the researcher, multiple ways of knowing, expanded validity practices, and shared power in the research process.

Undergraduate and graduate leadership education benefits from the inclusion of action research for several reasons. First, as a research method, its values and practices are congruent with those of 21st-century models of leadership. Leadership content and the research process are mutually reinforcing. Second, if leadership is about creating social change, then this method is not only an academic exercise of applying knowledge, it is also a change-making opportunity. Third, when students engage in action research, the four core processes of planning, acting, reflecting and observing (Kuhne & Quigley, 1997) challenge them to slow down, disintegrate learning processes, and reflect upon them intentionally. The research process makes evident what is frequently invisible, both in the learning processes for students and the nuances of change itself.

For over a decade, Saint Mary's College of California has offered a graduate degree in leadership that provides an innovative and practical education in the theories, perspectives, and practices of leadership (www .smcleadership.org). The graduate program is a 19-month cohort model in which students spend approximately 40% of their time in person and the balance in a highly interactive online learning environment. The program is designed for for-profit and nonprofit managers, public service professionals, educators, community organizers, entrepreneurs, direct service providers, and people from all sectors committed to practicing leadership for social change. The International Leadership Association's (ILA, 2009) "Guiding Questions: Guidelines for Leadership Education Programs" influence the ongoing development of the content and process of the program.

The sequence of graduate courses include building a learning community; values, ethics, and decision making; postindustrial leadership theory; foundations of justice; action research theory and practice; systems theory; building cross-cultural capacities; policy, leadership, and systemic change; social movements; and personal and organizational learning. Core texts for the program include Hall (2006), Heifetz, Grashow, and Linsky (2009), Korten (2006), Rosenberg (2003), and Wheatley (2006). The students' culminating project is a leadership action research project. It provides an example of how Fink's (2013) notion of application learning is useful in leadership education—both in its scaffolding of knowledge and action that build to the culminating project and in its inclusion of critical, creative, and practical thinking.

Graduate students are introduced to action research early in the program by reading action research articles in courses, listening to their peers in older cohorts discuss their projects, and by engaging in a series of reflective journal questions that slowly help the students determine a focus for their action research. These early explorations reflect triarchic thinking: What problem or opportunity do you see in your environment (critical thinking)? What people would be good collaborators with you in exploring a change strategy (creative thinking)? What is the timeline and stepwise planning for your research implementation (practical thinking)?

One third of the way through the graduate program students take a course focused on action research theory and practice. In the course, students acquire knowledge of action research methods and social change, design and implement a participatory change strategy, deepen library and research skills, and craft a strong draft of a literature review for their project proposals. The foundational texts for the course include *Participatory Action Research* (McIntyre, 2008) and *Handbook of Action Research: Concise Paperback Edition* (Reason & Bradbury-Huang, 2006). After this course, students then have several months to complete their proposal (and receive human subjects approval, when applicable), several months for implementing three cycles of the action research project (during which they are assigned to a faculty advisor for coaching and feedback), and then several more months to write the final project. The project guide and faculty advisors provide very specific guidance throughout the process.

Leadership development, innovation, and effectiveness—critical, creative, and practical thinking—are all challenged and strengthened by the action research process. Figure 3.1 identifies these four core processes (Kuhne & Quigley, 1997) and identifies when triarchic thinking is evident throughout.

As stated early in this chapter, application learning (Fink, 2013) is not only about critical, creative, and practical thinking, it is also about managing complex projects and developing performance skills. Action research reflects the full scope of application learning. Not only are students engaged in triarchic thinking, they are managing a multistakeholder project that spans several months and relies upon their affective, behavioral, and cognitive skills, and developing the performance skills such as group facilitation, presentations, and coalition building.

Saint Mary's College leadership graduate students have produced solid scholarship and lasting change through their action research projects. Recent foci have included developing a leadership curriculum for formerly incarcerated mothers, initiating a human rights antitrafficking campaign on a college campus, designing a sex education curriculum for developmentally disabled youth, addressing inequalities for female police officers, and exploring public policy options to reduce bullying. Through these efforts, students widen and deepen their leadership capacities, develop confidence in their ability to collaborate with others to create change, and foster the

Figure 3.1.   Core Processes of Action Research and Thinking

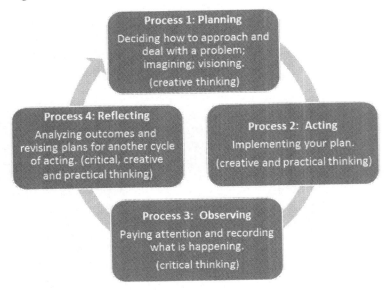

Source: Adapted from Kuhne & Quigley (1997).

humility to learn from unsuccessful attempts. Ultimately they can apply that which they have learned in the program to a practical need and desire in the real world. A similar outcome is also possible in cocurricular programs.

Service Learning and Leadership Learning.   Service learning and community service are increasingly linked to leadership education. Sometimes, service is an element of leadership education, and other times service programs are designed with leadership development as an outcome. High-quality academic and cocurricular service-learning programs have clearly defined learning objectives, intentionally designed service experiences that meet community-identified needs and goals, and intentional reflection and meaning making (Jacoby, 1996), and some models (e.g., Billig, 2009) incorporate youth voice throughout the process. Service learning follows the experiential learning cycle (Kolb, 1984) and can produce significant learning outcomes (Eyler & Giles, 1999). The term service learning is frequently reserved for credit-bearing academic experiences; it can be appropriately applied to cocurricular experiences when they meet the criteria (Jacoby, 1996). As such, service learning is the preferred term in this discussion.

Leadership education and service learning are mutually reinforcing educational strategies. In an analysis of the Cooperative Institutional Research Program (CIRP) data, Vogelgesang and Astin (2000) concluded that academic and cocurricular service learning can lead to growth in leadership outcomes, which they defined as leadership ability, leadership activities, and self-perceived growth in interpersonal skills. Recent findings from the Multi-Institutional Study of Leadership (Dugan, Kodama, Correia, & Associates, 2013) reveal that participation in community service is strong predictor of increasing students' leadership capacities including group-related skills, the development of personal commitment, resiliency in complex systems, and disrupting assumptions.

Dugan et al. (2013) extend best practices for service learning to include considerations of leadership education. For example, the manner of the service should be cohesive with the leadership theories being taught; critical reflection provides the link between acquired knowledge, direct experience, and meaning making; and the service experience must be processed in the specific context of leadership education (Dugan et al., 2013). The authors also suggest guiding questions for leadership educators related to professional development, program development, and applying a critical lens to service-leadership education. Many of these concerns are met in the following example.

The Catholic Institute for Lasallian Social Action (CILSA; www.stmarys-ca.edu/cilsa) at Saint Mary's College of California offers multiple community service and leadership development opportunities grounded in the theory and practice of service learning, the social change model of leadership, and Catholic Social Thought. Each year approximately 65 students commit to 300 hours of service and leadership development in CILSA programs and nearly 30% of the student body is enrolled in community engagement courses. One of CILSA's programs, the Micah Summer Fellowship Program, is the unit of analysis for this discussion of leadership education and application learning through critical, creative, and practical thinking.

The Micah Summer Fellowship Program provides undergraduates the opportunity to deepen their knowledge and practice of spirituality, leadership, social justice, community, and simple living. For eight weeks, Micah Fellows live together in a modest apartment in a housing development for formerly homeless families, work full-time at nonprofits in the Bay Area, share a modest food budget, participate in twice-weekly seminars and reflections with staff, and write an ongoing blog and papers linking their readings, seminar conversations, and living and serving experiences. The Micah Fellows curriculum includes *The Rich and the Rest of Us: A Poverty Manifesto* (Smiley & West, 2012), *Leadership for a Better World: Understanding the Social Change Model of Leadership Development* (Komives et al., 2009), and excerpts from texts such as *Where We Stand: Class Matters* (hooks, 2000) and *Globalization, Spirituality and Justice: Navigating the Path to Peace* (Groody, 2012). The program is designed to advance students' vocational and professional development and a growing awareness of their relationship to contemporary social problems.

As a tool for program or course review, leadership educators can utilize Fink's (2013) Taxonomy of Significant Learning as a set of evaluation benchmarks placed on a matrix. We could then ask ourselves to what degree and when and how do the different types of learning occur? Table 3.2 summarizes the broad learning outcomes of the Micah Program and offers specific examples of questions and activities that foster leadership development (critical thinking), innovation (creative thinking), and effectiveness (practical thinking).

The Micah Program is intentionally a complex leadership development experience. It involves students in all four of the high-impact learning practices that the Multi-Institutional Study of Leadership recommends for building leadership capacity (Dugan et al., 2013). Students engage in:

- sociocultural conversations with peers—both emergent and initiated by readings and conversations with staff facilitators,
- mentoring relationships—with supervisors and staff,
- community service—both direct service and capacity-building projects at local nonprofits, and
- membership in an off-campus organization—by becoming full-time staff members at their nonprofits.

Students are immersed in challenges and surrounded by support. The experience is also reflective of other elements of Fink's (2013) taxonomy of learning, particularly caring, integration, and human dimension.

Beyond Courses and Immersive Programs.   In addition to teaching credit-bearing courses and facilitating long-term experiences, leadership educators operate with various time constraints, in more and less structured environments, and with varying group sizes. The key to applying the action research and service-leadership immersion examples to other contexts is to consider how they reveal something new about application learning, triarchic thinking, and leadership development, innovation, and effectiveness. With this new knowledge in mind, opportunities for infusing these ideas in leadership education will emerge.

For example, faculty and staff are often in a position to assist students with resume development and interview preparation. Frequently, students have difficulty explaining the full significance of their leadership experiences because they have not had an opportunity to be reflective about them and may not have the language for that reflection. The following questions invite students to reflect with specific purpose: What content knowledge and education are necessary for this position, and how did you apply it? What have you learned about group development, problem-solving, creating change, and interpersonal skills through this work? How has your experience in this position influenced your developing sense of leadership? In conversation with students (or in a workshop setting), leadership educators can assist students to name their capacities and cultivate the ability to communicate their leadership development (critical thinking), capacity for innovation (creative thinking), and leadership effectiveness (practical thinking).

NEW DIRECTIONS FOR STUDENT LEADERSHIP • DOI: 10.1002/yd

Table 3.2 Mapping Thinking in Micah Summer Fellowship Program

| | Micah Summer Fellowship Program | | |
| | Questions and Activities Designed to Foster Leadership Capacities Through Forms of Thinking | | |
Selected Learning Outcomes	Leadership Development and Critical Thinking	Leadership Innovation and Creative Thinking	Leadership Effectiveness and Practical Thinking
Leadership	Choose two of the values (i.e., "7 Cs") of the social change model of leadership and observe how they are enacted in your nonprofit site. In what ways is the social change model evident or not?	Design an experience for your coworkers to learn about and foster the 7 Cs value of "congruence."	What practical steps will you take to encourage your Micah Fellow peers and yourself to engage in the 7 Cs value of "controversy with civility"?:
Social justice	Apply the Catholic Social Thought principle of "preferential option for the poor" to a policy issue currently in the news.	How do we create social justice in a way that avoids a flip-flop of power (that avoids the oppressed becoming the oppressor)?	What are the implications of the principles of Catholic Social Thought for your own life?
Community	Compare and contrast the community(ies) in which you were raised and the ones where you are now living and serving.	Draw an image of your interpretation of King's *Beloved Community*.	How will your community of six people live on a combined food budget of $90/week?

Note: For more information on the Social Change Model of Leadership Development (the "7 Cs") see Higher Education Research Institute [HERI] (1996) or Komives et al. (2009).

When leadership educators invest in understanding the complexity of the leadership learning, we take action, for example, staging assignments, creating culminating projects, or performing a program assessment using a matrix. Leadership educators are then in a stronger position to design and facilitate assignments and experiences that lead students confidently into increasing leadership complexity. Whether leadership educators operate in an academic or cocurricular setting, the need for such forethought and planning is critical.

The Macroscopic View: Pathways to Social Change and Triarchic Thinking

This volume assumes a theoretical orientation that posits that leadership, and therefore leadership education, is about social change. Leadership for social change is a "purposeful, collaborative, value-based process that results in positive social change" (Komives et al., 2009, p. xii). The model is premised on two foundations: that leadership is tied to social responsibility and the development of the common good, and that increasing individuals' self-knowledge concurrently builds their capacities to work with others (Higher Education Research Institute [HERI], 1996). The connection between leadership and social change is also evident in Preskill and Brookfield (2009) whose nine ways of learning to support leadership for social justice include elements of critical, creative, and practical thinking, which are presented in more detail in Chapter 1 of this volume.

The University of California Berkeley's Center for Public Service has developed *Pathways to Service and Social Justice* (Bishop, 2014) that maps six ways in which students' can exercise social change both as students and in the future. The pathways include activism, community-engaged/community-benefitting scholarship, direct service, philanthropy, policy/politics, and social entrepreneurship. Table 3.3 offers examples of how critical, creative, and practical thinking are utilized in each pathway to social change.

While these categories and examples are not intended to be exhaustive, descriptors such as these have multiple applications. They can assist students in differentiating multiple social change strategies, invite students to build capacities in all three types of thinking, and provide a point of reference for vocational development conversations.

Currently, service-learning professionals at the University of California Berkeley, Stanford University, and Saint Mary's College of California are collaborating to devise educational materials and assessment tools that will help students explore these pathways of social change and build skills and capacities that will enable them to participate successfully in their chosen social change strategy. These institutions recognize that a long-term commitment to leadership for social change benefits from additional habits of being. These include a commitment to self-reflection and learning,

Table 3.3 Leadership for Social Change and Ways of Thinking

	Leadership Development/Critical Thinking	Leadership Innovation/Creative Thinking	Leadership Effectiveness/Practical Thinking
Pathways to social change			
Activism: Involving, educating, and mobilizing individual or collective action to influence or persuade others	Fosters abilities to analyze, evaluate, and critique; assess multiple interpretations; explain results; predict future outcomes	Invites new ideas, questions, products, and perspectives; engages multiple forms of expression	Develops problem-solving and decision-making capabilities; supports action-oriented choices
Public-benefitting scholarship: Connecting or producing scholarship with public and/or private sector resources that responds to community-identified needs or concerns	Critiquing power and institutionalized oppression; doing social analysis of signs of the times	Building coalitions among diverse constituencies; employing various communication techniques	Maintaining focus and commitment; sustained engagement in a purpose and with a community
Direct service: Giving time, energy, and resources to address immediate community concerns or priorities	Analyzing formal and informal sources of data; building new models	Translating results into forms that are useful to a variety of audiences	Making scholarship real by acting on its implications
	Working to understand assets, goals, and needs of individuals and communities	Developing new approaches; creatively engaging others in the work	Adjusting tactics as needed; monitoring progress

(Continued)

Table 3.3 Continued

	Leadership Development/Critical Thinking	*Leadership Innovation/Creative Thinking*	*Leadership Effectiveness/Practical Thinking*
Philanthropy: Voluntarily redistributing resources by individuals and institutions	Evaluating multiple funding opportunities in light of organizational and/or personal values	Increasing awareness of the issues at hand and expanding financial support	Partnering with grantees for ongoing project development and possible redirection
Policy/Politics: Participating in the processes of democratic self-governance	Assessing claims; researching issues; developing forecasts	Working across sectors to design solutions and agreements; questioning core assumptions	Crafting campaigns that engage and educate; balancing practical concerns with equity goals
Social entrepreneurship: Creating or expanding organizational structures that adopt ethical and effective business practices and/or generating market-oriented responses to solve social problems	Scanning the environment to capitalize on emergent opportunities; predicting needs and goals	Creating products and processes that equally value people, profit, and planet Earth; actively seeking multiple stakeholders	Maintaining open posture toward change and effectiveness of policies, products, and strategies

comfort with ambiguity, communication and coalition building, and the ability to be visionary in times of rapid change. These are values and practices that are core to 21st-century models of leadership.

Conclusion: The Leadership Educator as Praxis Mentor

Teaching and learning leadership for social change is a complex process that is ultimately about creating lasting change in students (Fink, 2013), and in the groups and systems in which they operate now and in the future. Freire's (1994) notion of praxis—"Reflection and action upon [and with] the world in order to transform it" (p. 33)—is a powerful orientation for leadership educators. Praxis reflects the theory-to-practice orientation of the study of leadership, the cycles of action and reflection in action research, the reflection that accompanies service, and the collaborative process of change. Through praxis, educators and learners strive together to name their condition and craft plans for moving forward.

Whether fostering critical, creative, and practical thinking, or nurturing other types of learning, leadership educators at our best are praxis mentors. Praxis mentors not only engage in the challenge and support necessary to foster students' learning and development, they model the leadership practices they hope to engender. Leadership educators take on the challenges of teaching with intentionality. They observe themselves and interrogate the biases and preconceptions that frame their sense of leadership and change. They consider how their educational practices support students' leadership development, innovation, and effectiveness. They identify as learners and seek ongoing professional development. They maintain at least three perspectives at once: the microscopic, the macroscopic, and the mirror. They wade into leadership complexity and remain committed to the cycles of action and reflection necessary for promoting social change in themselves, their students, and the world around us.

References

Billig, S. H. (2009). Does quality really matter: Testing the new K–12 service learning standards for quality practice. In B. E. Moely, S. H. Billig, & B. A. Holland (Eds.), *Advances in service-learning research* (Vol. 9, pp. 131–157). Greenwich, CT: Information Age.

Bishop, M. (2014). *Pathways to service and social justice*. Unpublished manuscript. Moraga, CA: Saint Mary's College Symposium.

Brooks, A., & Watkins, K. E. (1994). A new era for action technologies: A look at the issues. In A. Brooks & K. E. Watkins (Eds.), *The emerging power of action inquiry technologies: New directions for adult and continuing education* (pp. 5–16). San Francisco, CA: Jossey-Bass.

Brown, J., & Isaacs, D. (2005). *The world café: Shaping our futures through conversations that matter*. San Francisco, CA: Berrett-Koehler.

Dugan, J. P., Kodama, C., Correia, B., & Associates. (2013). *Multi-Institutional Study of Leadership insight report: Leadership program delivery*. College Park, MD: National Clearinghouse for Leadership Programs.

Eyler, J., & Giles, D. (1999). *Where's the learning in service-learning?* San Francisco, CA: Jossey-Bass.

Fink, L. D. (2013). *Creating significant learning experiences: An integrated approach to designing college courses.* San Francisco, CA: Jossey-Bass.

Freire, P. (1994). *Pedagogy of the oppressed* (Revised 20th anniversary edition). New York, NY: Continuum.

Groody, D. G. (2012). *Globalization, spirituality, and justice: Navigating the path to peace.* Maryknoll, NY: Orbis Books.

Hall, B. P. (2006). *Values shift: A guide to personal and organizational transformation.* Eugene, OR: Wipf & Stock.

Heifetz, R. A., Grashow, A., & Linsky, M. (2009). *The practice of adaptive leadership: Tools and tactics for changing your organization and the world.* Boston, MA: Harvard Business Review Press.

Higher Education Research Institute (HERI). (1996). *A social change model of leadership development: Guidebook version III.* Los Angeles: University of California, Los Angeles.

Hooks, B. (2000). *Where we stand: Class matters.* London, UK: Routledge.

International Leadership Association (ILA). (2009). *Guiding questions: Guidelines for leadership education programs.* Retrieved from http://www.ila-net.org/communities /LC/GuidingQuestionsFinal.pdf

Jacoby, B. (1996). *Service-learning in higher education: Concepts and practices.* San Francisco, CA: Jossey-Bass.

Kolb, D. A. (1984). *Experiential learning: Experience as the source of learning and development.* Upper Saddle River, NJ: Prentice Hall.

Komives, S. R., Wagner, W., & Associates. (2009). *Leadership for a better world: Understanding the social change model of leadership development.* San Francisco, CA: Jossey-Bass.

Korten, D. C. (2006). *The great turning: From empire to earth community.* San Francisco, CA: Berrett-Koehler.

Kuhne, G., & Quigley, A. (1997). Understanding and using action research in practice settings. *New Directions for Adult and Continuing Education, 73,* 23–40.

McIntyre, A. (2008). *Participatory action research.* Thousand Oaks, CA: Sage.

Preskill, S., & Brookfield, S. D. (2009). *Learning as a way of leading: Lessons from the struggle for social justice.* San Francisco, CA: Jossey-Bass.

Reason, P., & Bradbury-Huang, H. (2006). *Handbook of action research: Concise paperback edition.* London, UK: Sage.

Rosenberg, M. B. (2003). *Non-violent communication: A language of life* (2nd ed.). Encinitas, CA: Puddledancer Press.

Rost, J. C. (1993). *Leadership for the twenty-first century.* Westport, CT: Praeger.

Smiley, T., & West, C. (2012). *The rich and the rest of us: A poverty manifesto.* New York, NY: SmileyBooks.

Sternberg, R. J. (1989). *The triarchic mind: A new theory of human intelligence.* New York, NY: Penguin.

Vogelgesang, L. J., & Astin, A. W. (2000). Comparing the effects of community service and service-learning. *Michigan Journal of Community Service-Learning, 7,* 25–34.

Wheatley, M. J. (2006). *Leadership and the new science: Discovering order in a chaotic world.* San Francisco, CA: Berrett-Koehler.

JENNIFER M. PIGZA is the academic chair of the graduate program in Leadership for Social Justice and associate director of the Catholic Institute for Lasallian Social Action at Saint Mary's College of California.

4

Integrating diverse conceptions of leadership across different disciplines, perspectives, and epistemologies is imperative if leaders are to operate in a global and networked world. Interdisciplinary and integrative leadership courses and digital learning communities are featured examples.

Integrative and Interdisciplinary Approaches to Leadership Development

Julie E. Owen

While the preceding chapters explored the role of cognitive processes in leadership development, this chapter posits that it is no longer sufficient for leaders to develop cognitive complexity in only one or two disciplines if they are expected to address complex problems. Rather, if leadership is going to address systemic social issues such as global poverty or environmental challenges, leaders must be capable of multimodal thinking and be educated in *interdisciplinary*, *integrative*, and *intentional* ways. Fink's (2003, 2013) taxonomy of significant learning positions integration, which encompasses interdisciplinary learning, learning communities, and connecting academic work with other areas of life, as one of the realms of significant learning. Exploring diverse conceptions of leadership across different disciplines, perspectives, and epistemologies is imperative if leaders are to operate in a global and networked world. Interdisciplinary and integrative leadership courses and digital learning communities are featured examples.

Leadership Development as Interdisciplinary Learning

There is an emerging consensus that leadership, specifically the emerging discipline of leadership studies, is interdisciplinary in nature (Day, Harrison, & Halpin, 2009; Komives, Lucas, & McMahon, 2013; Riggio, 2013; Riggio & Harvey, 2012). As Rost (1993) predicted in his seminal book *Leadership for the Twenty-First Century*:

> Looking at leadership through the lens of a single discipline has not worked well in the past and it will not work any better in the future. Indeed, a case could be made that the organizations and societies of the future, with their

NEW DIRECTIONS FOR STUDENT LEADERSHIP, no. 145, Spring 2015 © 2015 Wiley Periodicals, Inc., A Wiley Company
Published online in Wiley Online Library (wileyonlinelibrary.com) • DOI: 10.1002/yd.20123

collaborative, community, and global orientations, may not be hospitable to a concept of leadership that is grounded in only one academic discipline. (p. 182)

Although leadership educators should acknowledge that the study and practice of leadership has its roots in numerous disciplines—the study of persuasion in communication, of motivation and influence in psychology, of management and organizations in business, of social movements in history, to name a few—there is general agreement that leadership development now requires learning from multiple disciplines and perspectives. It is not enough to learn or practice leadership in isolation from context. Some argue that leadership development should adopt a *multi*-disciplinary approach to leadership because "it develops a shared understanding of differences and commonalities in leadership principles and practices across professions and cultures" (Komives et al., 2013, p. 6). Others prefer the terms *inter*-disciplinary or *trans*-disciplinary, which imply greater integration and connection across "different kinds of information, perspectives, and methods of inquiry and analysis—all in order to develop a more holistic understanding of a problem or issue" (Fink, 2003, p. 43).

There are multiple definitions and drivers of interdisciplinarity, yet all involve the integration of knowledge and modes of thinking from two or more fields of study for the purposes of addressing questions in ways that would not be possible through the lens of a single discipline (Boix Mansilla & Gardner, 1997; Haynes, 2003; Klein 1990, 2002, 2005). Klein (2005) cites three catalysts for the rise of interdisciplinarity, including the knowledge explosion that resulted in increasing fragmentation of knowledge into subspecialties; complex problems demanding people to draw on multiple sources and kinds of knowledge; and educational reform that embraced pedagogies such as problem-based learning, team teaching, and other collaborations across disciplines. The benefits of interdisciplinary approaches to curricular and cocurricular leadership education are many. The world needs leaders who can synthesize knowledge across seemingly disparate fields and draw conclusions by combining examples, facts, and theories from more than one field of study (Rhodes, 2010). Navigating the "permanent whitewater" of the rapidly changing world requires leaders and leadership educators who can integrate theory and application, scholarship and intuition, and tradition and innovation (Vaill, 1996).

Many leadership studies programs address interdisciplinarity by having required courses offered from a variety of different academic departments. For example, the Ohio State University offers an interdisciplinary undergraduate minor in Leadership Studies that "provides students with knowledge of leadership theories, principles, and concepts to better prepare for success in future professional roles" (http://leadershipcenter.osu.edu /about-us/leadership-studies-minor). The minor is structured to include course options from a myriad of departments including communication, engineering, kinesiology, management, military science, philosophy, psychology, public affairs, and sociology. Courses are clustered into four categories and students must take at least one course in each category, as well as complete a practical capstone experience. The categories include theories and principles of personal leadership, team and organizational leadership, community leadership, and ethics and diversity. In this manner, students are allowed choice and latitude in their selection of courses and can personalize their leadership studies degree to match their interests.

Interdisciplinary approaches to leadership education can be fraught with challenges. As students are exposed to wide variety of learning goals and diverse epistemological orientations to the nature and purpose of knowledge, it can be challenging to form a coherent framework about leadership studies. Without purposeful integrative assignments and reflection, students may struggle to articulate connections across disciplinary views of leadership. Students must be intentionally encouraged to integrate, interrogate, and synthesize learning from diverse perspectives or leadership learning may be disjointed and even erroneous.

Additionally, there are structural challenges to designing and maintaining an interdisciplinary leadership program. University and departmental structures such as curriculum committees may be challenging to navigate, and creating a coherent curriculum with shared learning goals and developmental approaches to leadership education may be impossible. Maintaining commitments across numerous departments can be challenging, especially when facing leadership or faculty transitions. Cocurricular leadership educators may wrestle with facilitating leadership theories and approaches outside of educators' own training and background and instead only design programs based on familiarity.

Despite these challenges, the news is not all grim. Interdisciplinary approaches to leadership education invite students to be "aware of complex interdependencies, able to synthesize learning from a wide array of sources, to learn from experience, and to make productive connections between theory and practice" (Nussbaum, 1997, p. 3). Chapter 1 of this volume offered examples of what deeper, more sustained leadership learning could look like. Interdisciplinarity is one lever for deeper learning. Roberts (2007) articulates the power of interdisciplinary leadership education and cross-campus partnerships to transform not only students, but the academy itself:

> Because the study of leadership is so dependent on many disciplines and perspectives, exciting possibilities arise—for example, could leadership educators actually help refine or create new models for the generation and integration of knowledge in the academy? . . . Such joint efforts between faculty and staff could demonstrate the power of curricular and co-curricular engagement that is likely to transform the quality of learning in collegiate education in the future. (pp. 35–36)

Leadership Development as Integrative Learning

In the last decade there have been movements to distinguish *interdisciplinary* approaches, which mainly focus on generalizing and connecting current forms of knowledge, with *integrative* approaches, which focus on constructing new knowledge and raising epistemological questions about the nature and sources of knowledge (Klein, 2005). Integration of learning, and of leadership learning, is necessary in order to move past the increasingly fragmented, piecemeal, and haphazard approaches to undergraduate education. However, there are a wide variety of approaches to integration, many of which intentionally connect processes of reflection and metacognition. The Association of American Colleges & Universities' (AAC&U) *Statement on Integrative Learning* (Huber & Hutchings, 2004) describes several hallmarks of integrative learning, including "connecting skills and knowledge from multiple sources and experiences; applying theory to practice in various settings; utilizing diverse and even contradictory points of view; and understanding issues and positions contextually" (p. 13). AAC&U has developed a rubric for assessing integrative learning that defines integrative learning "as an understanding and a disposition that a student builds across the curriculum and co-curriculum, from making simple connections among ideas and experiences to synthesizing and transferring learning to new complex situations within and beyond the campus" (Rhodes, 2010, p. 1).

Examples of integrative approaches include linked courses, integrated general education experiences, capstone projects, learning communities, team teaching, civic engagement, service learning, first-year experiences, bridge programs, and peer mentoring (Huber, Hutchings, & Gale, 2005). Many of these integrative approaches to learning have also been identified as high-impact practices (HIPs) in education that promote deep learning and self-reported personal and practical gains (Kuh, 2008). Each of these HIPs leverages faculty–student interaction, academic challenge, and active, collaborative learning. Additionally, many of these integrative approaches have been shown to positively affect leadership learning and development (Dugan, Kodama, Correia, & Associates, 2013). For more on HIPs in leadership development, see chapter 6 in this volume.

Effective leadership education should similarly incorporate these levers of integrative learning. Table 4.1 offers examples of how to link principles of integrative learning to leadership education and development.

Integrative approaches to leadership explicitly connect academic study with the rest of one's life. Integrative leadership development does not distinguish between curricular, cocurricular, and extracurricular. Indeed, Palmer and Zajonc (2010) assert that "integrative education aims to 'think the world together' than to 'think it apart', to know the world in a way that empowers educated people to act on behalf of wholeness rather than fragmentation" (p. 22). If leadership educators want to create leaders who make

Table 4.1   Connecting Hallmarks of Integrative Learning to Leadership Education and Development

Hallmarks of Integrative Learning	Example in Leadership Education and Development
Connections to experience— connects relevant experience and academic knowledge	Students should be able to *synthesize connections among experiences outside the leadership classroom* (including life experiences such as civic and off-campus involvement, family life, artistic expression, cocurricular experiences, and other academic experiences such as internships and study abroad) to *deepen understanding* of leadership and broaden one's own philosophy and approach to leadership.
Connections to discipline—makes connections across disciplines and perspectives	Students should be able to *combine examples, facts, and theories from more than one field or perspective of leadership study.* For example, student should understand when a behavioral approach to leadership might be more effective than an influence-based approach, and vice versa.
Transfer—adapts and applies skills, abilities, theories, or methodologies gained in one situation to new situations	Students should be able to *adapt and apply leadership skills, abilities, theories, or methodologies gained in one context to a new situation* in order to solve difficult problems or explore complex issues in original ways. For example, student learns resilience from leading a project that was unsuccessful and applies that resilience to a campaign for a campus leadership position.
Integrated communication— communicates in ways that enhance meaning and demonstrate the interdependence of language, thought, and expression	Student can communicate effectively across multiple formats and forms of expression—from visual, digital, evidence-based, written, and oral—and *adapt thoughts to diverse audiences and contexts.* For example, student prepares a digital portfolio to demonstrate leadership learning and includes multiple forms of evidence such as videos of a speech, a written paper, an artistic expression of an opinion, etc.
Reflection and self-assessment— demonstrates a developing sense of self as a learner, building on prior experiences to respond to new and challenging contexts	Student *recognizes that leadership development is a lifelong process and can evaluate changes in leadership learning over time,* recognize complex contextual factors such as organizational and ethical considerations, and plan for future development to increase leadership competence and confidence.

Source: Adapted from Rhodes (2010).

connections across silos, structures, and disparate activities, they need to be practicing integrative leadership development.

One example of an integrative approach to leadership development is the University of Minnesota's integrative leadership minor: http://www.lead ership.umn.edu/education/integrative_leadership_minor.html. The minor is designed to create integrative connections and "to train future leaders to bridge institutional, geographical and national boundaries to address social, economic and political challenges" (accessed at http://www.leadership.umn .edu/education/integrative_leadership_minor.html, para. 1). The program also aligns multiple campus and community partners including the Center for Integrative Leadership, a joint venture between the Humphrey School of Public Affairs, Carlson School of Management, College of Education and Human Development, and the School of Public Health. Courses and academic learning communities offer training in leadership theory and civic engagement, and conclude with a seminar to stimulate students to apply their knowledge by developing ideas to resolve real-world case studies. Laura Bloomberg, executive director, Center for Integrative Leadership, University of Minnesota, offers the following as rationale for the integrative leadership minor:

> We will never be able to solve our biggest societal challenges by working in silos. The future will require leaders who understand the need to work across disciplines and boundaries to craft solutions. This program has the potential to change the way we prepare those future leaders here at the University of Minnesota. (accessed at http://www.leadership.umn.edu/education /integrative_leadership_minor.html, para. 3)

Leadership Development as Intentional Learning

No leadership educator can be successful in today's educational climate without their ability to show impact. Intentionality is essential in the design of learning communities, in developmental advising and mentoring, in the use formative assessment to gauge student learning as it is happening, and use of summative assessment to inform future leadership learning. Palmer and Zajonc (2010) underscore the challenge of balancing intentionality and spontaneity:

> Integrative forms of teaching and learning must have clear intentionality and trajectory, employing pedagogical designs that will take us and our students somewhere worth going. ... Doing integrative education well depends on our capacity to hold a paradox: we must open free space for the unpredictable and enforce an educative order. (p. 39)

One way to consider intentionality in leadership learning is to ponder the question "leadership for what purpose?". Though there are many possible responses and in *Learning as a Way of Leading: Lessons From the Struggle for Social Justice*, Preskill and Brookfield (2009) note that any consideration of leadership learning is dependent on a number of dispositions, capacities, and public practices. Their nine learning tasks of leadership are presented in Table 4.2 with accompanying reflection questions that invite students of leadership to critically reflect on how they are putting learning at the center of their leadership efforts.

Intentionality need not occur at the expense of innovation. Indeed, leadership education should be "adventuresome, exploratory, and discovery-oriented," meaning we should be embracing change and innovation while simultaneously setting intentions (Palmer & Zajonc, 2010, p. 39). The optimal balance among thoughtful pedagogical design, scaffolded learning, and risk-taking is up to each leadership educator. Experimental, technology-infused, and experiential approaches can invite intellectual curiosity and leadership. Christensen (2000) describes how processes of "disruptive innovation" evolve from simple grassroots applications and result in transformative change. Similarly, Heifetz (1994), director of Harvard's Center for Public Leadership, describes leadership as adaptive work, stating that leadership is "mobilizing people to tackle tough problems" (p. 15). Many are answering the 'leadership for what purpose?' question with an avowal of leadership as the intersection of intentionality, innovation, and shared public problem solving. This view "flows from a growing disillusionment with traditional, top-down, hierarchical models that dictate to, rather than work with, real people in real communities trying to find solutions to real problems" (Longo & Gibson, 2011, p. 3).

Intentional approaches to leadership development are especially apparent in integrative online learning (Cambridge, Cambridge, & Blake Yancey, 2009). Universities such as Fort Hays State and Gonzaga University, among others, offer fully online majors, minors, and certificates in leadership studies. These programs go far beyond merely providing access to leadership studies content. Instead, they use a wide variety of digital tools to create virtual learning communities that allow students to personalize learning, connect in meaningful ways with peers and faculty, apply theory to practice through case studies and digital simulations, assess leadership growth and development, and more. As leadership educators work to prepare students to be responsive to global, national, and local concerns, and to work across sectors and disciplines, new approaches to inquiry and knowledge creation must be considered.

Conclusion

In the face of increasing disciplinary specialization, shifting student enrollment patterns, and the accumulation of complex problems, "fostering students' abilities to integrate learning—across courses, over time, and between campus and community life—is one of the most important goals and

Table 4.2   Critically Reflecting on the Learning Tasks of Leadership

Nine Learning Tasks of Leadership	Questions for Critical Reflection
Learning how to be open to the contributions of others	What leadership knowledge, skills, and habits have you learned from collaborating with others? How open are you to alternative perspectives and creating space for dialogue and deliberation? What happened the last time you engaged in deep listening rather than putting forth your own perspective?
Learning how to critically reflect on one's practice	How often do you consider (and react to) issues of power, power relations, and equitable distribution of power in your leadership? Where does hegemony come into play (i.e., the dominance of one way of thinking)? To what extent are you aware of how you and those you serve may internalize ideas, beliefs, and values that may be undermining democratic outcomes? How do you support the agency of others? How are you supporting colleagues or community members in gaining meaningful control over their own work, learning, and lives?
Learning how to support the growth of others	How are you increasing the capacity of others to be active participants in the life of their community, movement, or organizations? Where are you seeing silence or withdrawal happen? What strategies do you use to stay curious about the lives of others? To ask constructive questions? To learn the stories of your collaborators?
Learning how to develop collective leadership	Where are you challenging the myth of heroic, self-sufficient, and individualistic leadership? How are you working with others to create a shared vision? Are you willing to subordinate your own aims to the group's goals and interests?
Learning how to analyze experience	To what extent are your experiences shaped by forces under your control as opposed to forces that transcend your immediate circumstances? How does your understanding of your experiences change as you adopt different lenses for examining them? Which leadership experiences invite repetition and which encourage avoidance?
Learning how to question oneself and others	How do you move beyond asking rote questions to ones that invite discovery and wonder? How might you use questions to critique and assess shared accomplishments? How might you use questions to "unpack platitudes and deconstruct conventional wisdom"?

Table 4.2   Continued

Nine Learning Tasks of Leadership	Questions for Critical Reflection
Learning to live democratically	How is leadership (putting energies and talents toward collective goals) an inherent civic responsibility? How is leadership (participating fully and having an equal opportunity to influence the outcomes of deliberations) an inherent right? Where do you invite democratic dialogue, responsive to each community member's needs and concerns?
Learning to sustain hope in the face of struggle	How is hope a necessary precondition for social change? For leadership? How do you sustain hope over time? How do you use dissent to illuminate shortcomings and consequences of decisions? To what extent do you share examples of ordinary people doing extraordinary things?
Learning to create community	How does your community embody each of the principles described above? How are you harnessing the power of collective thought and action in order to transform society? How do communities invite redistribution of resources? Shared authority and accountability?

Source: Adapted from Preskill & Brookfield (2009).

challenges of higher education" (Huber & Hutchings, 2004, p. 13). Many leadership educators were perhaps attracted to leadership studies because leadership can be a kind of through-line or connection point for students across the fragmented landscape of higher education courses, online learning, cocurricular experiences, and career development. When done in intentional, integrative, and interdisciplinary ways, leadership education and development can be a synthesizing force that invites students to connect cognitive, affective, and leadership learning; to develop habits of mind that invite diverse perspectives and multiple lenses on any situation; to value the processes of discovery and inquiry; and to connect multiple theories to diverse practices and contexts.

References

Boix Mansilla, V., & Gardner, H. (1997). What are the qualities of disciplinary understanding? In M. S. Wiske (Ed.), Teaching for understanding: Linking research with practice (pp. 161–196). San Francisco, CA: Jossey Bass.

Cambridge, D., Cambridge, B., & Blake Yancey, K. (2009). Electronic portfolios 2.0: Emergent research on implementation and impact. Sterling, VA: Stylus.

Christensen, C. (2000). *The innovator's dilemma: When new technologies cause great firms to fail.* Cambridge, MA: Harvard University Press.

Day, D. V., Harrison, M. M., & Halpin, S. M. (2009). *An integrative approach to leader development: Connecting adult development, identity, and expertise.* New York, NY: Routledge.

Dugan, J. P., Kodama, C., Correia, B., & Associates. (2013). *Multi-Institutional Study of Leadership insight report: Leadership program delivery.* College Park, MD: National Clearinghouse for Leadership Programs.

Fink, L. D. (2003). *Creating significant learning experiences: An integrated approach to designing college courses.* San Francisco, CA: Jossey-Bass.

Fink, L. D. (2013). *Creating significant learning experiences: An integrated approach to designing college courses* (2nd ed.). San Francisco, CA: Jossey-Bass.

Haynes, C. (Ed.). (2003). *Innovations in interdisciplinary teaching (American Council on Education Series on Higher Education).* Westport, CT: Oryx.

Heifetz, R. A. (1994). *Leadership without easy answers.* Cambridge, MA: Harvard University.

Huber, M. T., & Hutchings, P. (2004). *Integrative learning: Mapping the terrain.* Washington, DC: Association of American Colleges & Universities and the Carnegie Foundation for the Advancement of Teaching.

Huber, M. T., Hutchings, P., & Gale, R. (2005, summer/fall). Integrative learning for liberal education. *peerReview, 7*(4), 4–7.

Klein, J. T. (1990). *Interdisciplinarity: History, theory, and practice.* Detroit, MI: Wayne State University Press.

Klein, J. T. (Ed.). (2002). *Interdisciplinary education in K-12 and college: A foundation for K-16 dialogue.* New York, NY: The College Board.

Klein, J. T. (2005, summer/fall). Integrative learning and interdisciplinary studies. *peerReview, 7*(4), 8–10.

Komives, S. R., Lucas, N., & McMahon, T. R. (2013). *Exploring leadership: For college students who want to make a difference* (3rd ed.). San Francisco, CA: Jossey-Bass.

Kuh, G. D. (2008). *High impact practices: What they are, who has access to them, and why they matter.* Washington, DC: Association of American Colleges & Universities.

Longo, N. V., & Gibson, C. M. (2011). *From command to community: A new approach to leadership education in colleges and universities.* Medford, MA: Tufts University Press.

Nussbaum, N. C. (1997). *Cultivating humanity: A classical defense of reform in liberal education.* Cambridge, MA: Harvard University Press.

Palmer, P. J., & Zajonc, A. (2010). *The heart of higher education: A call to renewal.* San Francisco, CA: Jossey-Bass.

Preskill, S., & Brookfield, S. D. (2009). *Learning as a way of leading: Lessons from the struggle for social justice.* San Francisco, CA: Jossey-Bass.

Rhodes, T. L. (2010). *Assessing outcomes and improving achievement: Tips and tools for using rubrics.* Washington, DC: Association of American Colleges & Universities.

Riggio, R. E. (2013). Advancing the discipline of leadership studies. *Journal of Leadership Educators, 12*(3), 10–14.

Riggio, R. E., & Harvey, M. (Eds.). (2012). *Leadership studies: The dialogue of disciplines.* Northampton, MA: Edward Elgar.

Rost, J. C. (1993). *Leadership for the twenty-first century.* Westport, CT: Praeger.

Roberts, D. C. (2007). *Deeper learning in leadership.* San Francisco, CA: Jossey-Bass.

Vaill, P. B. (1996). *Learning as a way of being: Strategies for survival in a world of permanent white water.* San Francisco, CA: Jossey-Bass.

JULIE E. OWEN is an associate professor of leadership and integrative studies and executive director of Social Action & Integrative Learning (SAIL) in New Century College at George Mason University.

5

This chapter examines humanistic ways of understanding learning; connects leadership learning to the concepts of personal competence, social competence, and caring; and introduces the model of emotionally intelligent leadership.

Valuing Human Significance: Connecting Leadership Development to Personal Competence, Social Competence, and Caring

Paige Haber-Curran, Scott J. Allen, Marcy Levy Shankman

It is often said that one has to be able to lead themselves before they can lead others. Further, there are many real-life examples of how someone's lack of self-awareness negatively impacts his or her ability to effectively work with and lead others. One's ability to know oneself serves as a key foundation from which to build strong relationships with others and is a cornerstone of leadership.

Relationships are central to any leadership process, and the development of intrapersonal and interpersonal competence facilitates healthy, reciprocal relationships that can ultimately lead to successful leadership. Thus, it is imperative that leadership educators devote considerable attention to helping students learn about themselves and others. Although the notions of personal competence (knowing oneself) and social competence (knowing others) seem simple in concept, they are not so easy in practice and indeed may be very difficult for youth who are learning daily about themselves and others. The development of personal and social competence takes considerable commitment and energy; it is promising to know that these areas of competence *can* be developed and can significantly influence one's ability to effectively lead (Goleman, 2005).

The purpose of this chapter is to examine the theme of valuing human significance within leadership education. The chapter first examines the concept of leadership with the lens of humanistic psychology. Next, it focuses on the areas of personal and social competence framed within the human dimension of Fink's (2013) taxonomy of significant learning.

New Directions for Student Leadership, no. 145, Spring 2015 © 2015 Wiley Periodicals, Inc., A Wiley Company
Published online in Wiley Online Library (wileyonlinelibrary.com) • DOI: 10.1002/yd.20124

The emotionally intelligent leadership (EIL) model is presented as a framework that captures many of the human dimensions of learning leadership discussed in the chapter, and the chapter concludes by highlighting three institutions that intentionally incorporate a focus on personal and social competence into their leadership education initiatives.

Leadership Through a Humanistic Lens

Conger (1992) describes leadership programs as focusing on four key areas: conceptual understanding, personal growth, skill building, and feedback. Programs with a focus on conceptual understanding are cognitive in nature (e.g., theory); personal growth programming focuses on the personal development and growth of the individual; skill-building programs are designed to develop specific leadership skillsets; and programs with a focus on feedback provide the learner with a new understanding of self, based on the perceptions of others. One could also look to the learning literature and map several theories from that domain onto Conger's model. Whereas Conger's *conceptual* model could connect with learning theories that focus on information processing, and *skill building* with behavioral approaches to learning, Conger's *personal growth* and *feedback* dimensions align with humanistic learning theories made popular by scholars such as Maslow (1943) and Rogers (1961). It is in this humanistic realm that we focus our attention in this chapter.

A concern for developing the whole person is not a new concept. Drawn from the teachings of Buddha, for more than 450 years the Jesuits have been concerned with developing the "whole person," described in Latin as *cura personalis*. Jesuits are interested in developing not only skilled and knowledgeable students, but are also interested in the individual better understanding the self. Although the word "humanism" has taken on different meanings, this chapter uses the term as Merriam and Caffarella (1999) suggest: "humanist theories consider learning from the perspective of the human potential for growth" (p. 256).

The roots of humanistic psychology and the concern for developing the whole person expressed by the Jesuits are reflected in the focus on developing the whole student apparent in higher education today (National Association of Student Personnel Administrators and the American College Personnel Association [NASPA/ACPA], 2004). The focus on developing the "whole student" can be seen in leadership programs that are designed to help students better understand their values, motivations, emotions, purpose, and goals.

In the leadership literature, much has been written on the concept of self-awareness. However, narrowing the focus solely on self-awareness minimizes the vast number of dimensions inherent in the concept of "self" and may do a disservice to the lifelong work of studying self (Avolio, 2005). Only in recent years have leadership scholars begun to dig deeper into this dimension of leadership development and focused on topics such as leadership identity, metacognition, moral reasoning, character, and self-efficacy (Bass, 2008; Day, Harrison, & Halpin, 2009; Komives, Owen, Longerbeam, Mainella, & Osteen, 2005). Chapter 2 of this volume describes some of these approaches in more detail.

The Human Dimension of Learning: Interpersonal and Social Competence

In addition to the inner, or personal, dimension of leadership development, it is imperative to also consider the social dimension of leadership. Leadership is a social phenomenon and interpersonal in nature, thus requiring engagement with others in the process of leadership through "initiating, building, and maintaining relationships with a variety of people who might differ from oneself in terms of age, gender, ethnicity, social class, or political agendas" (Hogan & Warrenfeltz, 2003, p. 79). Thus, there is a need to develop interpersonal or social competence, which can be viewed through multiple theories of learning (e.g., cognitive, social learning, constructivism), including behavioral skill building. Leadership development involves growth in one's knowledge, beliefs, skills, and ultimately behavior. For instance, one objective for skill development may be an increased ability to engage others in the movement, goal, or cause. This often requires that an individual be skilled in activities such as understanding what motivates others, recognizing others' strengths and needs, managing group dynamics, building meaningful relationships with others, managing conflict, and empowering and inspiring others. For example, a fraternity president tasked with eliminating hazing will have to be aware of group dynamics, navigate competing factions, and ultimately communicate a better reality to members. Or, a nonelected group leader of an academic project will need to quickly determine strengths of each member, communicate a clear vision, and empower team members to own their individual parts.

Discussed throughout this volume, learning about leadership is a multidimensional and complex process. Fink's (2013) taxonomy for significant learning presented in Chapter 1 highlights different forms of meaningful learning. One form of learning, the *human dimension*, clearly aligns with the personal and social aspects of leadership reviewed in the previous section. Concerned with the "important relationships and interactions we all have with ourselves and with others" (Fink, 2003, p. 44), the human dimension of learning prioritizes intrapersonal and interpersonal learning.

Importance of Learning About Self and Others

Many contemporary leadership frameworks emphasize the importance of *self* and *others*. Table 5.1 provides an overview of the components of select

Table 5.1   Contemporary Leadership Models With a Focus on Self and Others

Leadership Model	Focus on Self	Focus on Others
Emotionally Intelligent Leadership (Shankman et al., 2015)	Consciousness of self; emotional self-perception; emotional self-control; authenticity; healthy self-esteem; flexibility; optimism; achievement	Consciousness of others; displaying empathy; inspiring others; coaching others; capitalizing on difference; developing relationships; building teams; demonstrating citizenship; managing conflict; facilitating change
Social Change Model of Leadership (Higher Education Research Institute [HERI], 1996)	Consciousness of self; congruence; commitment	Collaboration; common purpose; controversy with civility
Adaptive Leadership (Heifetz, 1994)	Awareness of and ability to shift one's values, ways of viewing the world, and habitual ways of behaving	Ability to understand others' motivations, values, and capacities; ability to "read a group" and mobilize others
Five Exemplary Practices of Leadership (Kouzes & Posner, 2012)	Modeling the way	Inspiring a shared vision; enabling others to act; encouraging the heart
Relational Leadership Model (Komives, Lucas, & McMahon, 2013)	Awareness of one's values; trustworthiness; authenticity; self-esteem; open to difference; committed; optimistic	Empowering others; listening; working as a team; valuing others' contributions; developing common purpose
Servant Leadership (Greenleaf, 1977)	Self-awareness; foresight; healing oneself; visionary	Listening; empathy; persuasion; commitment to the growth of others; building community; healing others

leadership models often used with college students that align with a focus on self and others.

In addition to leadership models often used with college student populations, outcomes of personal and social competence are emphasized in other guiding documents for leadership education. Three such documents, highlighted in Table 5.2, are the Council for the Advancement of Standards

Table 5.2   Guiding Documents With Outcomes Related to Personal and
Social Competence

Guiding Document	Personal Competence Outcomes	Social Competence Outcomes
CAS Standards for Student Leadership Programs (CAS, 2012)	Realistic self-appraisal, self-understanding, & self-respect; identity development; commitment to ethics & integrity; spiritual awareness	Meaningful relationships; interdependence; collaboration; effective leadership
ILA's Guiding Questions: Guidelines for Leadership Education Programs (ILA, 2009)	Personal development; self-awareness; personal growth/change; renewal; spirituality; self in relation to others	Interpersonal skills; communication; group dynamics
AAC&U's Liberal Education and America's Promise: Essential Learning Outcomes (AAC&U, 2014)	Intercultural knowledge; ethical reasoning and action; skills for lifelong learning	Teamwork; communication; intercultural competence

in Higher Education (CAS, 2012) "Standards for Student Leadership Programs," the International Leadership Association's (ILA, 2009) "Guiding Questions: Guidelines for Leadership Education Programs," and the Association of American Colleges and Universities' (AAC&U, 2014) "Liberal Education and America's Promise: Essential Learning Outcomes."

Learning about oneself and others is "among the most significant experiences [students] have during college" (Fink, 2003, p. 44), as well as in high school. The literature on youth psychosocial and identity development identifies learning to know oneself and to know others as salient themes in students' development (Baxter Magolda, 2001; Chickering & Reisser, 1993; Kegan, 1982). Further, the process by which students develop a leadership identity, presented in Chapter 2 of this volume, involves the key developmental experiences of developing self (e.g., deepening self-awareness, building self-confidence, establishing interpersonal efficacy), building capacity in working with others in groups, and developing interdependent relationships with others (Komives et al., 2005). Through these developmental experiences, students' views of leadership and themselves become more complex, and students express greater capacity for relational leadership.

With such a strong emphasis on understanding self and others within models and frameworks of leadership, it is crucial for leadership education programs to include learning goals related to personal competence and social competence (see Table 5.2 for outcome areas). Leadership programs should provide opportunities for students to engage in personal exploration of their own values, strengths, emotions, perspectives, privileges, and identities. This exploration can provide a foundation from which students can

Table 5.3　Dimensions of Caring Applied to Leadership Education

Dimension of Caring (Fink, 2013)	Example Applied to Leadership Education and Development
Phenomena	Interest in leadership models and theories
Ideas	Curiosity about implications or assumptions of leadership concepts
Self	Excitement about one's own leadership potential or passions
Others	Interest in working with and learning from others
Process of learning	Passion about one's own leadership learning and development

Source: Adapted from Fink (2013).

develop effective and healthy competencies and behaviors to guide themselves and their leadership practice. Further, by providing opportunities for students to "better understand and interact with other people" (Fink, 2003, p. 45), leadership programs enable students to learn to understand and be aware of the values, motivations, emotions, needs, perspectives, and identities of others. This social awareness can lead to increased capacity to build more meaningful and authentic relationships with others and identify ways to motivate, influence, and empower others.

Connection to Caring

Another form of significant learning presented within Fink's (2013) taxonomy is caring. Although the main focus of this chapter is on the human dimension of learning, the learning category of *caring* is intricately connected to personal and social competence. Caring in the context of Fink's (2013) taxonomy involves the development of new feelings, interests, and values. Table 5.3 presents these dimensions of caring with examples related to leadership education.

Particularly since leadership learning can be a complex, developmental process involving challenges, deep commitment, and uncertainty (Heifetz, 1994; Komives et al., 2005), it is pivotal that leadership educators consider and focus on students' interest in, feelings for, and passion for leadership learning and development.

Emotionally Intelligent Leadership

Concepts of emotional intelligence and EIL are frameworks that capture many of the aspects of Fink's (2013) focus on the human dimension and caring as significant forms of learning. Emotional intelligence has received a great deal of attention in the popular and academic literature in recent years (Goleman, 2005; Mavroveli, Petrides, Rieffe, & Bakker, 2007; Salovey & Mayer, 1990). At its foundation, emotional intelligence is concerned with personal and social competence and encompasses "the ability to monitor one's own and others' feelings and emotions to use the information to guide one's thinking and actions" (Salovey & Mayer, 1990, p. 189). One framework of emotional intelligence emphasizes personal competence through the domains of self-awareness and self-management; a focus on social competence is reflected within the domains of social awareness and relationship management (Goleman, Boyatzis, & McKee, 2013). Research links emotional intelligence to leadership, and much of the research suggests that emotional intelligence more so than IQ, technical expertise, or advanced degrees is a significant factor contributing to one's leadership performance and success (Goleman et al., 2013).

Shankman, Allen, and Haber-Curran (2015) integrated the key concepts of emotional intelligence with contemporary leadership thinking to develop the model of EIL. The model encompasses three facets of development: consciousness of self, consciousness of others, and consciousness of context (Shankman et al., 2015). Embedded in the EIL facets are 19 capacities that equip individuals with the knowledge, skills, perspectives, and attitudes to achieve desired outcomes (Table 5.4).

EIL clearly aligns with Fink's (2013) human dimension of learning; at its core, EIL is based on the premise of personal and social competence.

Table 5.4   Emotionally Intelligent Leadership (EIL)

Consciousness of Self: Awareness of Your Abilities, Emotions, and Perceptions

Emotional self-perception: Identifying emotions and their impact on behavior
Emotional self-control: Consciously moderating emotions
Authenticity: Being transparent and trustworthy
Healthy self-esteem: Having a balanced sense of self
Flexibility: Being open and adaptive to change
Optimism: Having a positive outlook
Initiative: Taking action
Achievement: Striving for excellence

Consciousness of Others: Awareness of the Abilities, Emotions, and Perceptions of Others

Displaying empathy: Being emotionally in tune with others
Inspiring others: Energizing individuals and groups
Coaching others: Enhancing the skills and abilities of others
Capitalizing on difference: Benefiting from multiple perspectives
Developing relationships: Building a network of trusting relationships
Building teams: Working with others to accomplish a shared purpose
Demonstrating citizenship: Fulfilling responsibilities to the group
Managing conflict: Identifying and resolving conflict
Facilitating change: Working toward new directions

Consciousness of Context: Awareness of the Setting and Situation

Analyzing the group: Interpreting group dynamics
Assessing the environment: Interpreting external forces and trends

Source: Adapted from Shankman, Allen, & Haber-Curran (2015).

Learning associated with personal and social competence is embedded in the facets of consciousness of self and consciousness of others. The third facet of EIL, consciousness of context, may not appear to be directly aligned with the theme of valuing human significance, but it facilitates and supports students' understanding and expression of their leadership learning and their EIL. As students develop their capacities of personal and social competence, consciousness of context and the capacities of analyzing the group and assessing the environment enable individuals to go one step further in their decision-making and leadership competence by enabling them to look beyond themselves and others to consider the larger setting and situation in which they are leading. For example, a newly elected president of student government will need to quickly become aware of contextual factors that will affect his or her presidency (e.g., budget cuts/layoffs, social/ political issues, constituent concerns). These considerations will foster a deeper understanding of the leadership challenges ahead.

Fink's (2013) caring dimension of student learning is also captured in EIL. As students develop their leadership capacity, they are often discerning and strengthening their own interests, values, and purposes. Further, as students engage and lead in student groups they learn to connect their interests and values to a purpose or cause larger than themselves. A number of the EIL capacities capture the development of caring as it relates to leadership learning. The development of one's capacities of authenticity, initiative, achievement, displaying citizenship, and facilitating change, as examples, can lead to students' growth in their interests, passions, and values. As a result, students' learning about caring deepens, which can further motivate or support their personal and social competence and thus their capacity for EIL.

Leadership Program Spotlights

It is rare to find leadership programs that do not include at least some emphasis on personal and social competence. Programs that do this particularly well include a clear and intentional focus valuing human significance in the structure, design, and outcomes of the program. This section highlights two institutions that include a comprehensive, intentional, and cutting-edge focus on personal and social competence.

A Case-in-Point Approach: University of San Diego's Minor in Leadership Studies.   The University of San Diego's *Minor in Leadership Studies* (2014) prioritizes outcomes of personal and social competence across the curriculum. One of the courses, *Leadership and Practice of Presence,* adopts an experiential case-in-point and group relations approach to teaching and learning leadership and has a substantial focus on the development of personal and social competence (Getz, 2009). The course, which involves a three-day weekend intensive format, creates an environment and system that reflects and reproduces aspects of organizational life. This format creates a real-life case study that unfolds and is examined here and now; the faculty members encourage students to evaluate themselves and their interactions with others as these events progress.

Many of the primary learning goals of the course reflect outcomes of personal and social competence and include an emphasis on emotional intelligence. The learning goals include students' ability to (a) develop the personal skills, awareness, and discipline necessary to exercise leadership effectively; (b) gain a better understanding about how to access different parts of themselves to help them engage more effectively with others for more effective leadership; (c) identify and evaluate their own roles, social identities, assumptions, and behaviors related to the exercise of leadership and authority; and (d) articulate an awareness of their relationships with others, and demonstrate understanding and empathy across differences (social identity, personality, style, and approaches) (University of San Diego, 2014). To facilitate this learning, students complete two reflection papers connected to the learning goals of the course and participate in a facilitator-led small group where the students engage in reflection and discussion of application of the learning to themselves and their leadership practice.

Skill Building Across Contexts: University of Illinois' Leadership Center. The Illinois Leadership Center (ILC) aims to "help provide the 'experience you need for life' to be successful in your community, organizations, and relationships" and focuses on skill building in four areas— self-development, interpersonal development, organizational and group development, and transitional development (University of Illinois, 2014, Welcome Statement). Directly aligned with outcomes of personal competence, the self-development category includes the dimensions of self-awareness and self-management. Directly aligned with outcomes of social competence, the interpersonal development category includes the dimensions of relationship building, communication skills, ethical practices, and team development.

The outcomes of self-development and interpersonal development are evident across ILC's leadership programs. I-programs, which are day-long cocurricular programs, are centered on topics such as Insight (personal themes or talents), Intersect (interpersonal knowledge), and Integrity (ethical leadership). Individual workshops are offered on topics such as strengths at the personal and team levels.

The Center also offers a Leadership Certificate, which is a self-tailored leadership program combining cocurricular programs and curricular leadership offerings. In order to customize the certificate, participants develop a personal development plan where they identify personal leadership objectives and evidence measures across the four primary areas of leadership (e.g., self-development, interpersonal development, organizational and group development, and transitional development). Additionally, participants are paired with a leadership coach, who meets monthly with participants to refine and implement the goals outlined in the participant's personal development plan.

The *Minor in Leadership Studies* includes three foundational courses (theory, the interpersonal nature of leadership, and research), a culminating capstone course, and two electives. One elective, *Emotional Intelligence Skills*, is centered on personal and social competence. The course focuses on recognizing and understanding one's own emotions and the emotions of others. Additionally, there is a focus on assessing and improving one's own emotional intelligence and interpersonal skills including self-regulation, empathetic listening, communication, collaboration, teamwork, motivation, influence, conflict management, and managing change (University of Illinois, 2014).

Conclusion

This chapter began with the assertion that it is imperative leadership educators devote considerable attention to helping students learn about themselves and others. Linking Fink's (2013) taxonomy of significant learning, specifically the forms of human dimension and caring, to EIL details how personal competence (consciousness of self) and social competence (consciousness of others) are essential for college student leadership development. With the enhanced understanding of the setting and situation (consciousness of context), students have guideposts by which they can develop their self-knowledge and knowledge about others. When leadership educators approach their work with an eye to intentionally supporting student learning and caring, giving students opportunities to practice, and sharing feedback with students, they are modeling a critical aspect of leadership development—valuing human significance.

References

Association of American Colleges and Universities. (2014). *Liberal education and America's promise: Essential learning outcomes.* Retrieved from http://www.aacu.org/leap/vision.cfm

Avolio, B. (2005). *Leadership development in balance.* Mahwah, NJ: Lawrence Earlbaum Associates.

Bass, B. (2008). *The Bass handbook of leadership: Theory, research and managerial applications* (4th ed.). New York, NY: The Free Press.

Baxter Magolda, M. B. (2001). *Making their own way: Narratives for transforming higher education to promote self-development.* Sterling, VA: Stylus.

Chickering, A. W., & Reisser, L. (1993). *Education and identity* (2nd ed.). San Francisco, CA: Jossey-Bass.

Conger, J. (1992). *Learning to lead.* San Francisco, CA: Jossey-Bass.

Council for the Advancement of Standards in Higher Education (CAS). (2012). *CAS professional standards for higher education* (8th ed.). Washington, DC: Author.

Day, D. V., Harrison, M. M., & Halpin, S. (2009). *An integrative approach to leader development: Connecting adult development, identity, and expertise.* New York, NY: Routledge.

Fink, L. D. (2003). *Creating significant learning experiences: An integrate approach to designing college courses*. San Francisco, CA: Jossey-Bass.

Fink, L. D. (2013). *Creating significant learning experiences: An integrated approach to designing college courses* (2nd ed.). San Francisco, CA: Jossey-Bass.

Getz, C. (2009). Teaching leadership as exploring sacred space. *Educational Action Research, 17*(3), 447–461.

Goleman, D. (2005). *Emotional intelligence* (2nd ed.). New York, NY: Bantam Books.

Goleman, D., Boyatzis, R., & McKee, A. (2013). *Primal leadership: Learning to lead with emotional intelligence* (2nd ed.). Boston, MA: Harvard Business School.

Greenleaf, R. K. (1977). *Servant leadership: A journey into the nature and power of greatness*. Mahwah, NJ: Paulist Press.

Heifetz, R. A. (1994). *Leadership without easy answers*. Cambridge, MA: Harvard University Press.

Higher Education Research Institute (HERI). (1996). *A social change model of leadership development, guidebook III*. Los Angeles, CA: Author.

Hogan, R., & Warrenfeltz, R. (2003). Educating the modern manager. *Academy of Management Learning and Education, 2*(1), 74–84.

International Leadership Association. (2009). *Guiding questions: Guidelines for leadership education programs*. Retrieved from http://www.ila-net.org/communities/LC /GuidingQuestionsFinal.pdf

Kegan, R. (1982). *The evolving self: Problem and process in human development*. Cambridge, MA: Harvard University Press.

Komives, S. R., Lucas, N., & McMahon, T. R. (2013). *Exploring leadership: For college students who want to make a difference* (3rd ed.). San Francisco, CA: Jossey-Bass.

Komives, S. R., Owen, J. E., Longerbeam, S. D., Mainella, F. C., & Osteen, L. (2005). Developing a leadership identity: A grounded theory. *Journal of College Student Development, 46*, 593–611.

Kouzes, J., & Posner, B. (2012). *The leadership challenge* (5th ed.). San Francisco, CA: Jossey-Bass.

Maslow, A. H. (1943). A Theory of Human Motivation. *Psychological Review, 50*(4), 370–396.

Mavroveli, S., Petrides, K. V., Rieffe, C., & Bakker, F. (2007). Trait emotional intelligence, psychological well-being and peer-rated social competence in adolescence. *British Journal of Developmental Psychology, 25*, 263–275.

Merriam, S. B., & Caffarella, R. S. (1999). *Learning in adulthood: A comprehensive guide* (2nd ed.). San Francisco, CA: Jossey-Bass.

National Association of Student Personnel Administrators and the American College Personnel Association (NASPA/ACPA). (2004). *Learning reconsidered: A campus-wide focus on the student experience*. Author.

Rogers, C. R. (1961). *On becoming a person: A therapist's view of psychotherapy*. Boston, MA: Houghton Mifflin.

Salovey, P., & Mayer, J. D. (1990). Emotional intelligence. *Imagination, Cognition, and Personality, 9*(3), 185–211.

Shankman, M. L., Allen, S. J., & Haber-Curran, P. (2015). *Emotionally intelligent leadership: A guide for students* (2nd ed.). San Francisco, CA: Jossey-Bass.

University of Illinois. (2014). *Illinois Leadership Center*. Retrieved from http://www .illinoisleadership.illinois.edu/

University of San Diego. (2014). *Minor in leadership studies*. Retrieved from https://www .sandiego.edu/soles/academics/leadership-minor/

PAIGE HABER-CURRAN *is an assistant professor and program coordinator for the Student Affairs in Higher Education program at Texas State University.*

SCOTT J. ALLEN *is an associate professor of management at John Carroll University.*

MARCY LEVY SHANKMAN *is the director of Leadership Cleveland and Strategic Initiatives at the Cleveland Leadership Center.*

NEW DIRECTIONS FOR STUDENT LEADERSHIP • DOI: 10.1002/yd

Leadership educators can leverage high-impact experiences to enhance student leadership development. This chapter describes three key practices—sociocultural conversations with peers, mentoring, and membership in off-campus organizations—as levers of leadership learning. Illustrations of the practice in context and reflections from practitioners and students are also included. The chapter concludes with considerations of context, developmental readiness, and best practices of experiential education.

Connecting to Experience: High-Impact Practices for Leadership Development

Kerry L. Priest, Nicholas A. Clegorne

It is often said that experience is the best teacher. Experiential and active learning have long been the hallmarks of leadership education and development. The pursuit of significant leadership learning challenges educators to consider both the process and outcome of experience (Fink, 2013). In recent years, the theme of powerful pedagogies for leadership education has taken on new life as educators explore intersections between theories of learning and leadership development. Scholars and practitioners have asked important questions about not only what to teach but also how to teach it in pursuit of best-practices in leadership education (e.g., Eich, 2008; International Leadership Association [ILA], 2009; Jenkins, 2012; Owen, 2011). The nexus of *how* students learn, *what* educators teach, and what leadership is *for* has opened new spaces for conversation, scholarship, and professional development.

Student development literature documents the high value of educationally purposeful activities to student learning and development (Astin, 1993; Kuh, Kinzie, Schuh, Whitt, & Associates, 2005; Pascarella & Terenzini, 2005). In short, what students do in college matters. By extension the same could be asserted for youth: what students do in high school matters.

How do leadership educators create engagement in purposeful learning opportunities? The Association of American Colleges and Universities' (AAC&U) *Liberal Education and America's Promise* (LEAP) initiative advocates the use of high-impact educational practices in pursuit of essential

New Directions for Student Leadership, no. 145, Spring 2015 © 2015 Wiley Periodicals, Inc., A Wiley Company
Published online in Wiley Online Library (wileyonlinelibrary.com) • DOI: 10.1002/yd.20125

learning outcomes that prepare students for a complex, diverse, and changing world (AAC&U, 2007; Kuh, 2008). These high-impact practices are purposeful, proven strategies characterized by collaborative experiences in diverse contexts combined with feedback, reflection, and application of learning (Kuh, 2008). The purpose and outcomes of LEAP in many ways overlap the assumptions and values of the social change model of leadership development, which frames socially responsible leaders as individuals who are motivated to exercise leadership for the purpose of impacting change on behalf of others and for the benefit of society as a whole (Higher Education Research Institute [HERI], 1996; Komives, Wagner, & Associates, 2009). Table 6.1 outlines some of the commonalities found between these contemporary models of higher education learning and leadership development.

The Multi-Institutional Study of Leadership (MSL) investigates influences that shape socially responsible leadership capacity and other leadership related outcomes in college students (see www.leadershipstudy.net). The MSL reveals important findings about "what works" in leadership education; namely that pedagogy (the content and the way that content is delivered) is more important than program or platform (e.g., curricular vs. cocurricular format; Dugan, Kodama, Correia, & Associates, 2013, p. 5). More specifically, evidence confirms the value of several high-impact practices on building student leadership capacity: sociocultural conversations with peers, the development of mentoring relationships, membership in off-campus organizations, and community service (Dugan et al., 2013).

How can educators leverage these high-impact experiences to develop more effectively both leadership capacity and leadership efficacy? This chapter describes three of the four key practices (a detailed exploration of creating powerful community service and civic-engagement opportunities is found in Chapter 7 of this volume). Each description includes a profile illustrating the practice in a specific context and offers reflection from practitioners and students. The chapter concludes with considerations of context, developmental readiness, and best practices of experiential education.

Sociocultural Conversations With Peers.   Higher education's call to develop students' values and competencies of global citizenship challenges educators to develop courses, programs, and experiences exploring diverse cultures, life experiences, and varying world views (AAC&U, 2007; Kuh, 2008). How do students develop the capacity to understand self and others in order to create positive change for society? Evidence from MSL research suggests that the educational practice of sociocultural conversations with peers is the strongest predictor of socially responsible leadership capacity for students across demographic groups (Dugan et al., 2013; Segar, Hershey, & Dugan, 2008). Sociocultural conversations can take multiple forms, but generally include formal and informal dialogues with peers *about* differences, as well as interactions *across* differences (e.g., race/ethnicity, lifestyle, customs, social issues, political values, or religious beliefs). As

Table 6.1   Some Shared Facets of Higher Education Learning and Leadership Development

	Liberal Education and America's Promise (LEAP) Campaign (AAC&U, 2007) *A Guiding Vision and Framework for 21st-Century Education*	Social Change Model of Leadership Development (HERI, 1996) *A Contemporary Model of Student Leadership Development*
Purpose	• Develop college-educated workers, and more engaged and informed citizens. • Advance innovative and effective educational practices.	• Enhance student learning and development, specifically through increasing capacity for effective, socially responsible leadership. • Facilitate positive social change within institutions and communities.
Principles/Assumptions	• Learning should connect knowledge with choices and action. • Learning happens when students engage with "real-world" problems. • Learning should foster civic, intercultural, and ethical learning, with an emphasis on personal and social responsibility, in all fields of study.	• Leadership is a collaborative, relational process. The choices and actions of leaders impact broader groups and communities. • Leadership is about change; engaging problems to make a better world and more just society is the goal of leadership. • Equity, social justice, self-knowledge, personal empowerment, collaboration, citizenship, and service are important values for leadership.
Learning Outcomes	• Intellectual and practical skills • *Critical thinking, teamwork, communication, and problem solving* • Personal and social responsibility • *Civic engagement, engagement, intercultural competence, ethical action, lifelong learning*	• Consciousness of self • Congruence • Commitment • Collaboration • Common purpose • Controversy with civility • Citizenship • Change • Socio-cultural conversations • Mentoring • Off-campus experiences • Community Service
High-Impact Educational Practices	• Diversity/Global Learning, • Learning Communities, • Internships • Service/Community-Based Learning	

Source: Adapted from Association of American Colleges and Universities (2007); Dugan, Kodama, Correia, & Associates (2013); Higher Education Research Institute (1996); Komives, Wagner, & Associates (2009); Kuh (2008).

described in Chapter 2 of this volume, these discussions benefit from foundational skills such as active listening, social perspective taking (a cognitive skill reflecting the ability to take another person's point of view as well as accurately infer the thoughts and feelings of others), and critical self-refection (Dugan et al., 2013).

Fostering high-impact conversations require more than good teaching techniques; educators must also be self-reflective and participate in conversations about how their own identities, values, and beliefs shape their teaching and leadership practice. Chapter 1 of this volume offers reflective questions that can be used to enhance the critical consciousness of leadership educators. Students often look to the authority in the room for how to respond to tough questions or ideas, so it is vital that educators be aware of power dynamics (based on position or social identities) that exist in the conversation process. Educators should also be mindful that these conversations are not isolated to a single topic or workshop, but rather integrated throughout the curriculum (Dugan et al., 2013). The following profile provides a course-based example of facilitating high-quality sociocultural conversations connected to leadership.

Profile of Practice.   High-impact sociocultural conversations are the signature pedagogy used in Kansas State University's *LEAD 350: Culture and Context*, a core course for the undergraduate leadership studies minor. Students begin the semester learning key theoretical and conceptual frameworks that form both a foundation for understanding and language for talking about difference (e.g., Cullen's Core Concepts: social change model of leadership development, social construction, and ethnocentrism). Through self-reflection and dialogue, students are challenged to explore how the integration and intersectionality of identities (such as sexuality, race, religion, ability, and social class) influence their own and others' values, perspectives, and actions. Instructors utilize a variety of learning activities to help students engage with topics from multiple perspectives; for example, current events and case studies, simulations, cultural "immersion" assignments, and community-based research projects. A series of interviews conducted with participants from diverse campuses explored the effects of high-impact practices on leadership education. One of the participants, Leigh, a faculty instructor, explained how the use of current events helps students understand how to exercise leadership around contemporary social issues:

> These social conversations are happening all around us, every day. [For a given topic] I can find an example and say, 'Hey, this is something happening so let's talk about it. What do we do as leaders, what's our responsibility?' These conversations allow us to make sense of it together and come to the conclusion that there may not be one solution for this, but that process is what's important. We are not all going to agree ... but we are having the conversation ... That's how we are hopefully able to come to the best decision. (personal communication, May 13, 2014)

NEW DIRECTIONS FOR STUDENT LEADERSHIP • DOI: 10.1002/yd

For many students, *Culture and Context* may be the first time they have been asked to think about, let alone talk about, their beliefs regarding social issues and identities. Bethany, an undergraduate teaching assistant, said, "Students entering college don't know how to talk about issues. They don't know what language to use" (personal communication, May 13, 2014). She saw how students gained comfort and confidence as they learned to talk about difference. Reflecting on her own role as a peer educator, Bethany realized that "all of us have a story." This propelled her to ask and engage with questions like "What about our story helps us make sense of our beliefs about difference?" and "How does our background effect how we see the world?"

Riley, a student in the course, exemplified what Fink (2013) calls the human dimension of learning. He said, "I kind of came to the point where I realized, 'What I say right now has an impact on the way somebody feels about themselves.' [I] went from trying not to [make people mad], to [realizing] someone's feelings are at stake." The personal and social implications of his learning contributed to his growth as a leader. His advice to others: "It's tough, awkward, and uncomfortable, and it's not something you necessarily want to do readily. But when you push yourself, that's when you grow" (personal communication, May 13, 2014).

Meredith found it took preparation and courage to lead sociocultural conversations. As a teaching assistant, she learned the power of being a curious listener and asking questions. Her advice: "Don't be afraid to ask 'Why?'" (personal communication, May 13, 2014). Indeed, when educators create a safe environment for sociocultural conversations, they can more intentionally challenge students to search out the root of their beliefs—without judgment—for the sake of learning and leadership development.

Mentoring Relationships.   In classic literature, Mentor was a faithful guide and coach to king Odysseus' sons during the Trojan War (Garvie, 1994). In our modern world, it is easy to see a parallel in the characteristics of a trusted counselor assisting in the cultivation of leadership among youth and college students. The evolution of beliefs and practices of mentorship in the last century have mirrored those of leadership: moving from hierarchical, mentor-centric paradigms such as apprenticeship models to more learner-centered, relational approaches (Campbell, Smith, Dugan, & Komives, 2012).

MSL researchers defined a mentor as a person (i.e., faculty, staff, employers, family members, community members, or older peers) who "intentionally assisted the student's growth or connects the student to opportunities for career or personal development" (Dugan et al., 2013, p. 10). Mentoring as a process for leadership development has been explored and described in the contexts of public education (Middlebrooks & Haberkorn, 2009), undergraduate teaching assistant experiences (Odom, Ho, & Moore, 2014), and participation in a student-alumni mentoring program (Priest & Donley, 2014).

While mentoring has been linked to increased leadership efficacy and socially responsible leadership capacity in college students (Campbell et al., 2012; Jabaji, Slife, Komives, & Dugan, 2008), emerging research from the MSL revealed that the type of mentor with the most effect on leadership capacity varied by racial group (see Dugan et al., 2013). This suggests that close attention should be given to creating contexts for students to form relationships with a variety of adults and peers representing multiple social identities. Educators should be mindful to establish well-defined goals and outcomes that explicitly reflect mentoring for leadership development, and provide training to both mentors and mentees that surface and address personal, social, or institutional factors that help/hinder the mentoring processes (Dugan et al., 2013). The following profile illustrates multiple leadership mentoring opportunities fostered through the context of a living-learning community.

Profile of Practice.   The Residential Leadership Community at Virginia Tech is a living-learning program for first-year students. Around 200 students are organized into smaller communities of about 30 students each who live and learn together. The combination of academic coursework with cocurricular leadership experiences creates a fertile environment for students to form strong relationships with each other and with adult faculty and staff. Courses and programs are facilitated by a team of instructional faculty, student affairs professionals, position-based peer leaders (second-year students), and student interns.

Abby served in a peer leader role during her second year in the program. Abby's experience exemplifies the multiplicity of mentoring opportunities in the program and explicates the impact of faculty and peer relationships. Peer leaders serve multiple roles in the community, including serving as a classroom teaching assistant and bridging between faculty and students in the classroom. Abby shared about the mentoring relationship that emerged with her course instructor, Kelley:

> When I first met with Kelley ... I can't say that I was expecting to gain a mentor. She began asking me what I wanted out of the class, ways that I could be challenged, and goals that I wanted to reach. I think for some people, like Kelley, mentorship is just a way of life. I'm extremely thankful for this relationship, because she inspired me to pursue dreams I never would have thought I could achieve. (Personal communication, May 13, 2014)

Abby's experience as a mentee catalyzed her desire to be a peer mentor, and she developed into a meaningful mentor herself. She described this aspect of her peer leader role: "I thought it was interesting how I became a mentor for some freshmen. These relationships were very organic—it wasn't like we set up meetings or called ourselves the 'mentor and mentee,' but they were still meaningful" (personal communication, May 13, 2014). While the community was designed to include formal mentoring roles, Abby valued the organic ways in which those relationships developed. In this community, mentoring relationships provided her a space to develop as a leader *and* practice leadership. This reflects movement into the Generativity stage of the leadership identity development (LID) model as described in Chapter 2 of this volume. Abby learned deeper and more profound dimensions of leadership from this mentoring experience.

Membership in Off-Campus Organizations.   While university missions share an explicit call for application of learning to real-world problem (AAC&U, 2007), these aims may be overshadowed by implicit social, cultural, economic, and value-based homogeneity (or at the very least dominance or privilege) that exists in traditional higher education practice (Howard, 2011). Even well-intentioned, well-designed curricular and cocurricular university environments remain somewhat sterile substitutes for the almost boundless messiness and diversity of competing needs and values found in real-world spaces. MSL research has found that students' involvement in off-campus organizations contributes to socially responsible leadership development (Dugan et al., 2013). Examples of off-campus organizations may include non-profits, unions, religious groups or churches, parent–teacher associations, community action groups, and more. Additionally, these findings imply that off-campus involvement may better serve students' diverse needs, especially for students of color (Dugan et al., 2013).

Chapter 4 highlights the integrative nature of leadership education and offers insights into leveraging learning from lived experiences. What if leadership educators looked to lived, off-campus experiences to shape their curriculum, rather than vice versa? When the narrative of development emphasizes and values off-campus involvement, it legitimizes students' experiences and encourages meaningful connections to leadership. For example, discussions about off-campus experiences can be integrated into advising meetings, sociocultural conversations, and in-class reflections. Surfacing patterns in preferences of off-campus involvement can reveal implicit or explicit messages of legitimacy that may discourage on-campus involvement. Troubling identity politics of involvement can be a powerful move to a more socially just campus and global community (Dugan et al., 2013). The following profile illustrates the value of student-initiated involvement in a community-based service organization.

Profile of Practice.   Staff and volunteers at the YMCA at Washington State University deliver a variety of programs to support meaningful change in individuals and communities. Sarah, the former CEO of this program, observed a difference between students who became involved in YMCA programs on their own versus those who did so as a requirement for a course or cocurricular service credit. She said:

> When visiting our program sites, I noticed a difference in the engagement of students who chose to serve the community as a part of our team, as opposed to those who were assigned to complete a service-learning assignment with

us; often the Y was the only program that fit into their demanding schedules. Service becomes more than a class assignment as students begin to understanding the complex needs of the community and identify as active citizens creating real change in the lives of our youth, families, and athletes. (Personal communication, May 15, 2014)

Sarah went on to say that students who participated in reflection, mentoring, and additional training and development opportunities remained more engaged in Y programs and openly explored connections to academic coursework, their personal values, and possible social innovations to meet evolving community needs. Sarah cited one student in particular named Ashley who drove in from a neighboring university to join the Y's volunteer team. "She found the Y during her freshman year, [and] then went on to become a volunteer and program coordinator … and later volunteered to serve the Campus Y movement as a national officer" (personal communication, May 14, 2014).

Educators are well served to identify and promote involvement in organizations like the YMCA, as well as provide both structured and organic opportunities for reflection and application of experience. Off-campus involvement not only provides students the opportunity to see and exercise leadership in the "real" world, but can also be a source of support and development for students who may not identify strongly with the dominant on-campus culture(s) or organizational structures.

Considerations for Integrating High-Impact Practices

Many high-impact experiences can happen naturally; for example, a conversation over coffee, a trusted friendship developed through a living group, or meaningful off-campus work experience. However, the power of these pedagogies is in the meaning making fostered through intentional design and delivery. Here are three areas for educators to consider as they seek to integrate high-impact practices.

Context.   Leadership programs do not exist in isolation. Just as individual learning and development is situated within multiple, overlapping social contexts and communities (Lave & Wenger, 1991), so are leadership courses and programs situated within multidisciplinary and curricular platforms. Employing high-impact experiential practices creates space to explore the interconnected nature of varying contexts (e.g., classroom, campus, and civic), and also invites critical inquiry into relations of power and privilege, access to opportunities, and discursive characteristics that both help and hinder leadership development in these contexts. One analytical tool for such inquiry is the model of leadership contexts, which offers a framework for examining leadership processes through the lens of historical, contemporary, and immediate contexts (Wren & Swatez, 1995). Additionally, the social change model (SCM) of leadership development

Table 6.2 Contextual Questions for High-Impact Experiences
• What historical and contemporary events have impacted our community, university, program, and people? How do these inform or connect to the need for leadership education and development?
• What contexts have shaped our program's values and norms? Do our stated values line up with our lived practices?
• Are we an inclusive community? In what ways do our current goals and structures create or inhibit opportunities for participation?
• Do we provide opportunities for students to explore the contexts and situations that shaped their beliefs and values?
• Can our students articulate a purpose for their leadership? Does that purpose reflect a connection between individual, group, and societal values?

provides a useful framework examining interactions between individual, group, and societal values (HERI, 1996; Komives et al., 2009). Drawing from these models, Table 6.2 outlines key questions to help educators recognize various contextual contributions, and thus design more nuanced and intentional practices to foster student learning.

Developmental Readiness. High-impact practices for leadership education may be considered counternormative, in that they challenge students' paradigms of traditional teaching and learning (Howard, 1998). How students respond to and engage with these practices may depend on their developmental readiness, which includes both motivation and ability to learn (develop) new knowledge, skills, abilities, and attributes for leadership (Hannah & Avolio, 2010). Recognizing developmental influences has implications for sequencing program content and pedagogies (Dugan, 2013). Chapter 2 of this volume provides a more extensive discussion of developmental readiness for leadership learning. An exploration of student development literature related to moral development (e.g., Kohlberg, 1981), self-directed adult learning (e.g., Baxter Magolda, 2001; Kegan & Lahey, 2010), and identity development (e.g., Chickering & Reisser, 1993) also offers valuable insights.

The LID model (Komives, Longerbeam, Owen, Mainella, & Osteen, 2006; Komives, Owen, Longerbeam, Mainella, & Osteen, 2005) can be utilized as an analytical tool to understand students' developmental readiness. As noted in Chapter 2 of this volume, LID is a stage-based model which describes increasingly complex conceptualizations of leaders and leadership, as well as developmental influences. Using the LID to assess developmental readiness should be engaged with a nonpejorative attitude toward the stages. For example, stage 4 of the model (Leader Differentiated in which views of leadership are expanded beyond positional to be non-positional and process) is not "better" than stage 3 (Leader Identified in which leadership is viewed as positional and hierarchical), but understanding the stage with which a student chooses to identify can help design more intentional conversations, mentoring interactions, and service experiences. It can also

Table 6.3   LID-Based Questions to Assess Developmental Readiness

- What LID stage(s) do our faculty and staff identify with? What are the implications of this on program design and delivery?
- What LID stage(s) do our students typically identify with? How does this inform our understanding of students' needs?
- How can our courses, relationships, and other programming support or challenge students' views of self and leadership over time?

Table 6.4   Applying Principles of Experiential Education to Leadership Education Practice

NSEE Principle	Self-Reflection Questions
Intentionality	• Do we have clear learning objectives that are accessible to all parties involved? • Are we encouraging that certain viewpoints of leadership be adopted (e.g. is your intent to get all student to stage 6 of the LID)? Are we transparent in the purpose of every activity that you have students complete?
Preparedness and Planning	• How are we ensuring that program participants are ready for your experiences? • Do we have an application process or orientation program to ensure preparedness? How does/could this impact accessibility to our program and how will we mitigate any lack thereof?
Authenticity	• How will we ensure that you activities are meaningful in a real-world context? • What external resources or personnel could be engaged to help design such experiences?
Reflection	• Have we created opportunities for students to reflect? • How often and through what media will refection be available? • How will we help student to understand the value of reflection (e.g., not just "busy-work"?)
Orientation and Training	• How will students, faculty, staff, and outside partners be organized and given the space to be aligned with the program's goals and recognize their roles? • How will we provide continuing development to ensure consistent delivery of high-impact practices?
Monitoring & Continuous Improvement	• What are the goals and benchmarks of our program? How will we use goals and benchmarks to drive improvement, but remain flexible to student needs?
Assessment & Evaluation	• How are we documenting processes and outcomes? • How will we use this information to evaluate high-impact practices and the program as a whole?
Acknowledgement	• How do we acknowledging students' progress through engagement in these practices? • How are we acknowledging the program's development?

Source: Adapted from National Society for Experiential Education (NSEE) (2013).

help better draw out teachable moments from reflection about off-campus experiences. For example, a student who identifies with LID stage 3 (believing that leaders are different than followers fundamentally) may view a youth group leader who values group decision making or appreciative inquiry as weak or disorganized. A student who identifies with LID stage 4 may view the same group leader as considerate and empowering. In this way, the LID model provides a tool for making meaning of different perspectives. Table 6.3 features several leadership identity questions to assess developmental readiness.

Experiential Learning Principles.   The National Society for Experiential Education's (NSEE) eight principles of good practice offer a useful guide for designing and implementing high-impact practices (NSEE, 2013). More detail about each practice is available at the society's website (http://www.nsee.org/8-principles). Table 6.4 outlines specific questions to serve as starting points for application to a leadership course or program.

Conclusion

This chapter discussed the value of connecting to experience through high-impact educational practices; highlighted examples of high-impact practices in curricular, cocurricular, and community-based settings; and raised critical questions for consideration when designing courses or programs for varied learners and contexts. Leadership education has been described as a pedagogy of practice. That is, teaching and program facilitation is in itself an act of leadership. The use of experiential pedagogies is an opportunity to exercise socially responsible leadership for and with our students, colleagues, and peers in our own institutional and community contexts.

References

Association of American Colleges and Universities (AAC&U). (2007). *College learning for the new global century: A report from the National Leadership Council for Liberal Education & America's Promise.* Retrieved from: http://www.aacu.org /leap/documents/GlobalCentury_final.pdf

Astin, A. W. (1993). *What matters in college? Four critical years revisited.* San Francisco, CA: Jossey Bass.

Baxter Magolda, M. B. (2001). *Making their own way: Narratives for transforming higher education to promote self-development.* San Francisco, CA: Jossey-Bass.

Campbell, C. M., Smith, M., Dugan, J. P., & Komives, S. R. (2012). Mentors and college student leadership outcomes: The importance of position and process. *The Review of Higher Education, 3*(4), 595–625. doi:10.1353/rhe.2012.0037

Chickering, A. W., & Reisser, L. (1993). *Education and identity* (2nd ed.). San Francisco, CA: Jossey-Bass.

Dugan, J. P. (2013). Scholarship and research updates: Developmental readiness—framing the extant literature. *Concepts & Connections, 19*(3), 18–20.

Dugan, J. P., Kodama, C., Correia, B., & Associates. (2013). *Multi-Institutional Study of Leadership insight report: Leadership program delivery.* College Park, MD: National Clearinghouse for Leadership Programs.

Eich, D. (2008). A grounded theory of high-quality leadership programs: Perspectives from student leadership development programs in higher education. *Leadership & Organization Studies, 15,* 176–187. doi:10.1177/1548051808324099

Fink, L. D. (2013). *Creating significant learning experiences: An integrated approach to designing college courses.* San Francisco, CA: Jossey-Bass.

Garvie, A. F. (Ed.). (1994). *Homer: Odyssey.* Cambridge, UK: Cambridge University Press.

Hannah, S. T., & Avolio, B. J. (2010). Ready or not: How do we accelerate the developmental readiness of leaders? *Journal of Organizational Behavior, 31,* 1181–1187. doi:10.1002/job.675

Howard, A. (2011). Privileged pursuits of social justice: Exploring privileged college students' motivation for engaging in social justice. *Journal of College and Character, 12*(2), 1–14. doi:10.2202/1940-1639.1774

Howard, J. P. (1998). Academic service learning: A counternormative pedagogy. *New Directions for Teaching and Learning, 73.* doi:10.1002/tl.7303

Higher Education Research Institute (HERI). (1996). *A social change model of leadership development guidebook: Version III.* Los Angeles, CA: Author.

International Leadership Association (ILA). (2009). *Guiding questions: Guidelines for leadership education programs.* Retrieved from http://www.ila-net.org/communities /LC/GuidingQuestionsFinal.pdf

Jabaji, R., Slife, N., Komives, S., & Dugan, J. (2008). Mentoring relationships matter in developing student leadership. A publication of the National Clearinghouse for Leadership Programs. *Concepts & Connections, 15*(4), 7–8.

Jenkins, D. M. (2012). Exploring instructional strategies in student leadership development programming. *Journal of Leadership Studies, 6*(4), 48–62. doi:10.1002/jls.21266

Kegan, R., & Lahey, L. L. (2010). From subject to object: a constructive-developmental approach to reflective practice. In N. Lyons (Ed.), *Handbook of reflection and reflective inquiry: Mapping a way of knowing for professional practice* (pp. 433–449). New York, NY: Springer.

Kohlberg, L. (1981). *The philosophy of moral development* (Vol. 1). San Francisco, CA: Harper & Row.

Komives, S. R., Longerbeam, S. D., Owen, J. E., Mainella, F. C., & Osteen, L. (2006). A leadership identity development model: Applications from a grounded theory. *Journal of College Student Development, 47,* 401–418. doi:10.1353/csd.2006.0048

Komives, S. R., Owen, J. E., Longerbeam, S. D., Mainella, F. C., & Osteen, L. (2005). Developing a leadership identity: A grounded theory. *Journal of College Student Development, 46,* 593–611. doi:10.1353/csd.2005.0061

Komives, S. R., Wagner, W., & Associates. (2009). *Leadership for a better world: Understanding the social change model of leadership development.* San Francisco, CA: Jossey-Bass.

Kuh, G. D. (2008). *High-impact educational practices: What they are, who has access to them, and why they matter.* Washington, DC: Association of American Colleges and Universities.

Kuh, G. D., Kinzie, J., Schuh, J. H., Whitt, E. J., & Associates. (2005). *Student success in college: Creating conditions that matter.* San Francisco, CA: Jossey-Bass.

Lave, J., & Wenger, E. (1991). *Situated learning: Legitimate peripheral participation.* Cambridge, UK: Cambridge University Press.

Middlebrooks, A. E., & Haberkorn, J. T. (2009). Implicit leader development: The mentor role as prefatory leadership context. *Journal of Leadership Studies, 2*(4), 7–22. doi:10.1002/jls.20077

National Society for Experiential Education (NSEE). (2013). *Eight principles of good practice for all experiential learning activities.* Retrieved from http://www .nsee.org/8-principles

Odom, S. F., Ho, S. P., & Moore, L. L. (2014). The undergraduate leadership teaching assistant (ULTA): A high-impact practice for undergraduates studying leadership. *Journal of Leadership Education, 13*(2), 152–161. doi:10.12806/V12/A2

Owen, J. E. (2011). Considerations for student learning in leadership. In S. Komives, J. P. Dugan, J. E. Owen, & Associates (Eds.), *The handbook for student leadership development* (2nd ed., pp. 109–133). San Francisco, CA: Jossey-Bass.

Pascarella, E. T., & Terenzini, P. T. (2005). *How college affects students: A third decade of research.* San Francisco, CA: Jossey-Bass.

Priest, K. L., & Donley, S. (2014). Developing leaders for life: Outcomes from a collegiate student-alumni mentoring program. *Journal of Leadership Education, 13*(3), 107–117. doi:1012806/V13/I3/A2

Segar, T. C., Hershey, K., & Dugan, J. P. (2008). Socio-cultural conversations: The power of engagement across difference. *Concepts & Connections, 15*(4), 9–10.

Wren, J. T., & Swatez, M. J. (1995). The historical and contemporary contexts of leadership: A conceptual model. In J. T. Wren (Ed.), *The leader's companion: Insights on leadership through the ages* (pp. 245–252). New York, NY: Free Press.

KERRY L. PRIEST *is an assistant professor in the Staley School of Leadership Studies at Kansas State University.*

NICHOLAS A. CLEGORNE *is an assistant professor in the Department of Agricultural, Leadership, and Community Education and director of the Residential Leadership Community at Virginia Tech.*

7

This chapter explores the use of powerful pedagogies such as service-learning, cultural immersion, and community-based research to enhance leadership development. Four key principles are presented that describe how leadership educators can facilitate community-based learning in a way that creates an optimal learning environment for students, while also engaging ethically with individuals and organizations in the community.

Connecting to Communities: Powerful Pedagogies for Leading for Social Change

Wendy Wagner, Patricia Mathison

The previous chapter describes three high-impact practices that leverage leadership learning. This chapter explores additional powerful pedagogies such as service-learning, cultural immersion, and community-based research as ways to enhance leadership development. Civic engagement is an important feature of many leadership development programs, in part because it helps address *why* to do leadership development, but also because it can address *how* people do leadership. Leadership is not a practice that can be learned in the abstract, but through concrete experiences connected to meaning making. Working collaboratively to address real social and environmental issues is a powerful way for students to come to experience the ambiguity and complexity of leadership processes. When implemented well, these programs have been connected to increased leadership capacity and leadership self-efficacy (Dugan, Kodama, Correia, & Associates, 2013) and increased self-motivation to learn (Eyler & Giles, 1999; Jacoby, 1996).

Fink (2003) describes service learning as an integrative pedagogy where "students are encouraged to find and create connections between what they are learning in class and the activities of the larger community in which they live" (p. 44). These engaged learning models create two challenges for the leadership educator: (a) how to design programs that maximize student learning from these experiences and (b) how to also attend to the needs of the community, giving community partners a strong voice rather than acting upon them without fully understanding how those actions fit into their bigger picture.

New Directions for Student Leadership, no. 145, Spring 2015 © 2015 Wiley Periodicals, Inc., A Wiley Company
Published online in Wiley Online Library (wileyonlinelibrary.com) • DOI: 10.1002/yd.20126

A recent review of research findings indicated symptoms of a "civic malaise" in today's citizenry (The National Task Force on Civic Learning and Democratic Engagement, 2012, p. 6). An alarming proportion of Americans do not see themselves as having the responsibility or efficacy for civic engagement. In response to these findings, the Association of American Colleges and Universities (AAC&U) issued a call to action for higher education to connect college learning to democratic citizenship (The National Task Force on Civic Learning and Democratic Engagement, 2012). Leadership educators have long claimed a role in "creating leaders for a diverse and democratic society" (Allen, Astin, Astin, Burkhardt, & Cress, 2000, p. v). This commitment today is perhaps even more critical.

The Alignment of Leadership and Civic Learning Outcomes

Leadership development and civic engagement are concepts that intertwine in ways which enhance both. Civic engagement practices such as service-learning and community-based research give students a context and pedagogy through which to learn leadership in more transformational ways. Likewise, learning collaborative leadership values and skills prepares students to engage in the community more sensitively and effectively, "Effective leadership is an essential ingredient in positive social change" (Allen et al., 2000, p. iv).

While community engagement has been shown to enhance learning across the disciplines (Eyler & Giles, 1999; Mitchell, 2008), the alignment of learning objectives between the development of socially responsible leadership and civic participation is particularly clear. Leadership in today's rapidly changing world demands the ability to work collaboratively with colleagues from diverse backgrounds, address change in interconnected systems, and make decisions amid ambiguity (Heifetz, 1994; Komives, Lucas, & McMahon, 2013; Komives, Wagner & Associates, 2009). Many leadership educators recognize that the classroom is a fairly sanitized place for students to wrestle with what are actually quite complex, "messy" social problems. Community-based learning has the potential to give students experiences that will challenge their ability to simultaneously consider the influence of social systems, local history, cross-cultural dynamics. At the same time it can also challenge them to address their own assumptions about working with others, where knowledge lies, and how to engage in a leadership process. Service learning "is a pedagogy immersed in the complexities and ambiguities of how we come to make sense of ourselves and the world around us" (Butin, 2005, p. 98).

As noted elsewhere in this volume, numerous professional associations have connected aspects of civic engagement to desired leadership learning objectives. The Council for the Advancement of Standards (CAS) for Higher Education includes among its dimensions for student learning a sense of civic responsibility and social responsibility (CAS, 2012). Similarly, civic learning objectives typically include a leadership aspect. The AAC&U's framework of knowledge and skills needed for democratic engagement includes learning goals familiar to leadership educators: collaborative decision making, compromise, collaboration, civility, mutual respect, seeking and being informed by multiple perspectives, ethical integrity, and the ability to navigate both formal and informal political systems (Association of American Colleges and Universities [AAC&U], 2005).

Both the leadership and the service-learning research provide evidence to support leadership learning from community engagement. Recent research from the Multi-Institutional Study of Leadership (MSL) has indicated that community engagement is one of the four strongest predictors of leadership growth (Dugan et al., 2013). In other studies, service and service learning have been shown to correlate positively with increases in leadership, self-efficacy, clarification of values (Astin, Vogelgesang, Ikeda, & Yee, 2000), moral development, cultural awareness, tolerance for diversity (Finley, 2012), increased collaboration, interdependence, self-awareness, identity development, commitment to ethics and integrity, and greater complexity in the analysis of social problems, their causes, and potential solutions (Eyler & Giles, 1999; Mitchell, 2008). It is no wonder that early research on model leadership programs for young adults reported that 77% included service or volunteer placement, making it one of the top five leadership development practices of these programs (Allen et al., 2000).

Even if the evidence linking service experiences with leadership development was not clear, service learning would still be a worthy pedagogical option for the same reasons it is a powerful practice in any discipline. It fosters active, applied learning and expands students' self-motivation to learn (Butin, 2006). As noted in Chapter 6, service learning is also among the AAC&U's High Impact Practices (Kuh, 2008), which are learning strategies that have been shown to be useful pedagogy for all students, while correlating with even greater positive results for historically underserved students such as first-generation students and students of color.

Types of Community-Based Learning

Community-based learning is an umbrella term that includes a variety of pedagogical activities, all of which are rich contexts for learning collaborative leadership. Table 7.1 provides types of community-based learning activities.

Given that each of the forms of community-based learning has the potential to be an excellent context for leadership development, this chapter expands upon how leadership educators can facilitate community-based learning in a way that creates an optimal learning environment for students while also engaging ethically with individuals and organizations in the community. We offer the following four principles as general guidelines.

NEW DIRECTIONS FOR STUDENT LEADERSHIP • DOI: 10.1002/yd

Table 7.1   Types of Community-Based Learning Activities

Service learning	Community service combined with intentionally designed instruction, focusing on critical, reflective thinking and civic responsibility. Mutually beneficial partnerships give students opportunities to apply academic knowledge and skills in a real context, while addressing local needs. Service can be direct, students are on-site, interacting with community members, or indirect, with students working off-site on deliverables like lesson plans or marketing campaigns.
Critical service learning	Critical service learning is differentiated from traditional service learning by its focus on social justice and its goal to reveal and disrupt the social inequalities that are perpetuated by social institutions (Mitchell, 2008).
Community-based research	Research projects developed jointly between faculty and community organizations such that both benefit. When students are involved in the projects, it also facilitates student learning of social issues, research methods, and civic values. See Chapter 3 of this volume for examples of action research.
Advocacy	Sharing persuasive information through presentations, writing, or multimedia to political and corporate leaders or the general public, educating about a social issue and advocating actions that will address the root causes that contribute to the problem.

Principle 1: Critical Reflection.   As has been described in Chapters 2 and 3 of this volume, the importance of reflection on experience is a foundational concept to any form of experiential learning. High-quality reflection has been shown by the service-learning research to be absolutely necessary for reaching the desired outcomes of service-learning and of community-based research (Eyler & Giles, 1999; Strand, Cutforth, Stoecker, Marullo, & Donohue, 2003).

The pedagogy of community engagement values *critical* reflection, which challenges students to question assumptions that support social injustices in our communities and in our leadership groups. Critical reflection asks students to apply their experience to contemplate hard questions related to the nature of inequality: Why is economic stratification linked to racial groups? Why do multicultural groups still conform to the leadership norms of the majority culture? Critical reflection connects not only service and personal meaning making, it also connects to a greater understanding of the role of history, social norms, political power, and our own roles in holding up systems of inequality (Mitchell, 2008; Rhoads, 1997).

Critical reflection also requires students to examine their own assumptions and mental maps. They deepen their own self-awareness as they are asked to examine their interpretation of interactions with the community, questioning whether other interpretations might be valid.

Engagement in the community, paired with critical reflection, helps student leaders expand their understanding of sociocultural differences.

Their perception shifts from simply noticing differences to have awareness of systems of privilege and oppression at work. Opportunities to discuss these observations in diverse groups have been shown to be the greatest predictor of socially responsible leadership (Dugan et al., 2013).

Intentional critical reflection should be central to the design of a community-based leadership development initiative, never an afterthought. Program planning should include considerations for the tone and context in which students will be challenged to think more deeply about the nature of social injustices. Opportunities to dialogue with others about their different perspectives on sociopolitical issues should be embedded. Education related to how to engage in those discussions sensitively should be addressed.

NCLC 395: Leadership and Group Dynamics is a community-based learning course taught at George Mason University that uses a critical thinking framework to foster deeper, critical reflection about both community experiences and leadership processes. Working with a local affordable housing community, student teams develop and implement projects that address the community's identified needs. The five written reflection assignments use the critical thinking framework developed by Brookfield (2012) to challenge students to address the assumptions embedded in their observations. The Brookfield framework is also modeled in the classroom through weekly group discussions and adapted as follows:

- Describe the critical incident at hand. (This question was adjusted each week to focus attention on the topic at hand: group development, roles that they and others played in leadership processes, decision-making or problem-solving processes being used, etc.)
- What assumptions are being made here? By others? By me?
- What other reasonable explanations are there?
- How could I find out more?

Regular use of this framework proved a useful process for helping students to reflect more deeply on how they have interpreted other people's comments and actions (student group members and community members), and the assumptions they may have made about their intentions. The critical thinking structure gave students a way to articulate their observations with less fear of offending classmates. The ongoing use of a structured examination of assumptions helped students develop a habit of questioning whether their interpretations might be distorted by their own, often identity-based, frame of reference. Discussions were intentionally developmental, moving from "lighter" conversations like observations of how tasks were differentiated and assigned to the tone and inclusiveness of their group meetings, to a candid conversation about the way gender expectations were unfairly influencing the group dynamics of some student teams.

NEW DIRECTIONS FOR STUDENT LEADERSHIP • DOI: 10.1002/yd

Table 7.2   Types of Impact From Community-Based Learning

Impact on Student	Impact on Community	Unintended Harm
Students gain from the experience, learn more about the social issue, and enhance their learning.	Community experiences positive social change through the engagement of students and input from the community.	Projects that have the best intentions for positive social change but create challenges or burden for the community partner.

Principle 2: Ethical Practice in the Community.   As educators connect more thoughtfully with the community, learning from community partners, there is an inherent responsibility to create opportunities that are ethical, just, and utilize community voice and perspective. There are a number of challenges associated with creating a mutually beneficial partnership where power is shared and engagement is both meaningful and purposeful for all involved.

Community-based initiatives are an opportunity to model socially responsible leadership by demonstrating respect for community members' knowledge and experience by giving them significant control regarding the nature and direction of the project. Consistent issues facing engaged educators are how to create campus–community partnerships based on shared trust, without creating an unhealthy dependency, avoiding unintended harm (Jones & Palmerton, 2010). In other words, how to assess true impact on community? In an effort to capture our impact, three types of impact should be considered: impact on the community, impact on individual, and unintended harm, as seen in Table 7.2.

Critical examination of many service initiatives reveals that they often have greater focus on student impact and do not adequately address the community impact and potential for unintended harm. One example of this imbalance can be found in the typical alternative break program. Many institutions across the United States offer alternative break experiences, week-long service trips that educate students about a variety of social issues. Consider the experience of the community organization that hosts alternative break students from multiple institutions throughout the year to support an afterschool program, a common scenario. The students learn to work collaboratively to create lesson plans and serve as mentors. Unfortunately though, the institutions rarely work together, so each week the afterschool students experience a different set of mentors and disjointed lesson plans. The Haiti Compact (n.d.), comprised of five universities and the national nonprofit *Breakaway*, is an example of attempts to address this problem. The Compact fosters more deliberate coordination among alternative break programs in Haiti following the earthquake there. Members of the Compact share their research on community needs and assets with each other, and report their progress on ongoing projects.

Student efforts to address disaster relief are another common example. Each time a natural disaster occurs, service offices on campus become inundated with student leaders interested in volunteering, providing/ coordinating donation efforts and creating student groups and organizations in response. Students, and occasionally staff, don't always realize that disaster response requires a certain skill set. Students arriving on-site take away space and resources for those that do have the training and skills to be of greater assistance and response. Similarly, donated items given with good intentions but little critical thought (stuffed animals and perishable food) divert space and staff resources to attend to the sorting and storage of donations rather than the disaster itself.

Leadership educators have a role to play in encouraging this civic-minded spirit while adding in a dose of reality that even the most thoughtful approaches could indeed be more harmful than purposeful. We must encourage thoughtful dialogue and integrate more critical reflection. What are we assuming is needed here? What are the potential negative consequences to that action? Where can we go to learn more before acting?

Ultimately, community-based learning experiences can help leaders learn that the end goal is not simply having performed the service itself. These initiatives can teach valuable lessons about the difference between attending to needs and addressing the root causes of the problem; the importance of context (e.g., poverty in Washington, DC, is addressed differently and results in different needs than poverty in Appalachia); and the need to understand the political, economic, and cultural differences of communities engaged.

Principle 3: Pursue Sustained Partnerships Rather Than One-Time Projects. Approaching community-based initiatives with the goal to establish a sustained partnership is one of the best ways to address both ethical community engagement and student leadership development. "I think a great partnership is when you stop saying *my* students. They're *our* students. What are *our* needs? We share these things in common, so let's go for it" (Sanby, Ikeda, Cruz, Holland, & Rice, 2007, p. 4).

It can be a risk for a community partner to get involved in community-based learning, as they are often dealing with less reliable students, faculty or staff that are absent from the experience, and campuses that are consistently creating new projects for students that may only be at their organization for more than twenty hours. The amount of training for students to be able to do the work can take a large part of a volunteer coordinator's time.

According to the Community Voices Study (Sanby et al., 2007), focus groups of community partners described several challenges of working with campus service programs, which included the need for faculty involvement; the need for more collaboration in curriculum planning and learning goals; adequate orientation to the organization's mission and clients; more focus on evaluation, feedback, and assessing impact; less focus on tracking service hours; and flexibility beyond the confines of the academic calendar.

Student leaders engaging in community work need advising and support in order to conceive their work as not simply provide service hours, but helping organizations build capacity. The stronger the relationship the community partner has with the educator and the students, the stronger the program will be for all involved. As the relationship is established, all parties better understand the challenges, the program and expectations, and can continue to improve upon the work. These kinds of relationships build over time.

Student leadership development is also better addressed through ongoing partnerships. A sustained partnership, with a history and intended future, is better than one-day service projects when the learning goals for students are to develop mature interpersonal relationships, collaborate on shared goals, establish and sustain trust, navigate conflict and power politics, assess impact, and make strategic plans.

George Mason University has an ongoing partnership with the community center of an affordable housing neighborhood across the street from campus. Students are involved in program planning for children, teens, adults and seniors, provide tutoring, and do environmental projects like a community garden. Faculty members from several departments and students in a living-learning community all have ongoing projects and a close relationship with the community center director. The ongoing nature of this campus/community relationship means students in course-based and cocurricular programs are able to build upon the work of previous Mason students. They gain a deeper understanding of the complexities of creating change as they understand the long-term story of the projects they work on. As personal relationships grow over the years, faculty and staff have an ever-clearer understanding of the director's mission and vision and how they can support her. They also have developed a deep respect for her expertise and frequently invite her to campus as a guest speaker.

Principle 4: Design Programs That Address the Developmental Nature of Leadership and Civic Engagement.   Just as leadership development happens incrementally over time, so does the complexity with which students are able to consider social problems and engage with others in addressing them. "As the service-learning movement has evolved, many proponents are defining greater nuances between kinds of service experiences, levels of student responsibility, scale of issues addressed, learning outcomes sought, and the impact of engagement on community partners" (The National Task Force on Civic Learning and Democratic Engagement, 2012, p. 60).

Many leadership development programs are already designed around students' developmental readiness in terms of both cognitive complexity and interpersonal skills ranging from emerging leader to capstone program designs. Leadership programs that involve civic work should also be designed around civic developmental considerations. A particularly relevant model is McTighe Musil's *Faces/Stages of Citizenship* (2003) that describes

Table 7.3   Faces/Stages of Citizenship and Approaches to Community

Exclusionary	The community is defined as only one's own social circles. Students are disengaged from civic involvement.
Oblivious	The community is a resource to mine. Students are detached from civic activity.
Naïve	The community is a place to be engaged in activities. Students have no understanding of the community's history or cultural influences.
Charitable	The community is a space that needs assistance. Attention is put on deficiencies rather than assets the community may also have. Students become involved in order to feel good about being a helper, focusing on how much was given rather than on what the impact on the community was. While well intentioned, civic actions are based on the assumption that one's own perspective is normal, implying that the goal of service is to help *them* become more like *us*.
Reciprocal	The community is a resource to empower and be empowered by. Students see value in multiple perspectives, have increasing intercultural competence, and understand the community's specific history of inequalities.
Generative	The community is an interdependent resource with potential and possibilities. Students are able to analyze the interconnectedness of social issues and social systems in order to work collaboratively with others to address the root causes of inequality and other community problems.

Source: Adapted from McTighe Musil (2003).

students' shifting mental models for the meaning of community and their roles as citizens (see Table 7.3).

Design Programs With Developmentally Appropriate Learning Goals. While it may seem counterintuitive for a community-based leadership development program to choose *not* to engage students in service, some programs dedicated to ethical community practice and student development have students take no community action in their early involvement with the program. For example, while George Washington University's Human Services and Social Justice program is committed to engaging students in community action, particularly in leadership courses, the introductory course does not involve service. In this course, students learn about community first: city political structures, the culture of each of the eight DC Wards, and the history behind some of the city's most pressing issues. Students attend neighborhood council meetings and meet with local leaders to discuss the city's greatest social and environmental issues and how community leaders are already working to address them. Subsequent courses in the program are able to build from this knowledge base (Human Services & Social Justice Program, n.d.). In this way, the *learning* dimension of service learning comes before the service activity, helping to ensure that when students eventually do engage in the community it comes from an informed place.

Design Programs That Feature Prolonged Student Engagement and Multitiered Student Leadership Roles.   In alignment with the need to consider student development, there is a general movement in campus civic programs toward longer term student engagement. When students have the opportunity to work with a local organization over a period of time that expands beyond the academic semester, they are more likely to truly understand the issues and assets of the agency, to explore the limits and possibilities of work responsive to the structural conditions that the agency exists to address, and build the commitment to lifelong engagement in service of social change (Mitchell, 2008).

Campus service projects that do not include students as stakeholders with valid contributions to make have been critiqued (Zlotkowski, Horowitz, & Benson, 2011). The Bentley Service program described by Zlotkowski et al. (2011) provides an example of student-led service programs. The program has several tiers of positions, each with increasing complexity of responsibility. Two overall student coordinators monitor the alignment of all programs with the center mission. Student project managers guide individual service initiatives, facilitate orientation and reflection sessions.

Engaging students in the creation of service projects rather than providing programs for them to participate in fosters greater leadership outcomes. However, the training and ongoing support for these students is critical to program success. In order to ensure ethical community engagement and quality learning experiences for student participants, attention to both student leadership and civic development should be at the forefront of selecting students for these leadership roles (Cochrane & Schill, 2013).

Conclusion

Both the service-learning and the leadership research are clear—community engagement pedagogy can foster transformative learning on many learning objectives related to leadership. However, the research is also clear that these programs must be designed and implemented well in order to achieve those outcomes (Butin, 2006; Eyler & Giles, 1999; Jacoby, 1996). We encourage leadership educators to familiarize themselves with the abundant literature on community-based pedagogy.

References

Allen, K. L. Astin, A. W., Astin, H. S., Burkhardt, J., & Cress, C. M. (2000). *Leadership reconsidered: Engaging higher education in social change.* Ann Arbor, MI: W.K. Kellogg Foundation.

Association of American Colleges and Universities (AAC&U). (2005). *Liberal education and America's promise: Excellence for everyone as a nation goes to college.* Washington, DC: Author.

Astin, A. W., Vogelgesang, L. J., Ikeda, E. K., & Yee, J. A. (2000). *How service learning affects students.* Los Angeles: Higher Education Research Institute, University of California.

Brookfield, S. D. (2012). *Teaching for critical thinking: Tools and techniques to help students question their assumptions.* San Francisco, CA: Jossey-Bass.

Butin, D. W. (2005). *Service-learning in higher education: Critical issues and directions.* New York, NY: Palgrave Macmillan.

Butin, D. W. (2006). The limits of service learning in higher education. *The Review of Higher Education, 29*(4), 473–498.

Cochrane, A., & Schill, H. M. (2013). Learning through service: Structures that promote student leadership. *Deepening Community Engagement in Higher Education: Forging New Pathways, 29,* 29–40.

Council for the Advancement of Standards in Higher Education (CAS). (2012). *CAS professional standards for higher education* (8th ed.). Washington, DC: Author.

Dugan, J. P., Kodama, C., Correia, B., & Associates. (2013). *Multi-institutional study of leadership insight report: Leadership program delivery.* College Park, MD: National Clearinghouse for Leadership Programs.

Eyler, J., & Giles, D. E. J. (1999). *Where's the learning in service-learning?* San Francisco, CA: Jossey-Bass.

Fink, L. D. (2003). *Creating significant learning experiences: An integrated approach to designing college courses.* San Francisco, CA: Jossey-Bass.

Finley, A. (2012). *Making progress? What we know about the achievement of liberal education outcomes.* Washington, DC: Association of American Colleges and Universities.

Haiti Compact. (n.d.). *The compact model.* Retrieved from http://haiticompact.org/learn/the-compact-model/

Heifetz, R. A. (1994). *Leadership without easy answers.* Cambridge, MA: Harvard University Press.

Human Service & Social Justice Program. (n.d.). Retrieved from http://humanservices.columbian.gwu.edu

Jacoby, B. (Ed.). (1996). *Service-learning in higher education: Concepts and practices.* San Francisco, CA: Jossey-Bass.

Jones, S. R., & Palmerton, A. (2010). How to develop campus-community partnerships. In B. Jacoby & P. Mutascio (Eds.), *Looking in, reaching out: A reflective guide for community service-learning professionals* (pp. 163–184). Boston, MA: Campus Compact.

Komives, S. R., Lucas, N., & McMahon, T. R. (2013). *Exploring leadership: For college students who want to make a difference* (3rd ed.). San Francisco, CA: Jossey-Bass.

Komives, S. R., Wagner, W., & Associates. (2009). *Leadership for a better world: Understanding the social change model of leadership development.* San Francisco, CA: Jossey-Bass.

Kuh, G. D. (2008). *High-impact educational practices: What they are, who has access to them, and why they matter.* Washington, DC: Association of American Colleges and Universities.

McTighe Musil, C. (2003, spring). Educating for citizenship. *peerReview, 5*(3), 4–8.

Mitchell, T. D. (2008, spring). Traditional vs. critical service-learning: Engaging the literature to differentiate two models. *Michigan Journal of Community Service Learning, 14*(2), 50–65.

Rhoads, R. A. (1997). *Community service and higher learning: Explorations of the caring self.* Albany: State University of New York Press.

Sanby, M., Ikeda, E. K., Cruz, N. I., Holland, B., & Rice, K. L. (2007). *Community voices: A California Campus Compact study on partnerships.* San Francisco: California Campus Compact.

Strand, K. J., Cutforth, N., Stoecker, R., Marullo, S., & Donohue, P. (2003). *Community-based research and higher education: Principles and practices.* San Francisco, CA: Jossey-Bass.

The National Task Force on Civic Learning and Democratic Engagement. (2012). *A crucible moment: College learning and democracy's future.* Washington, DC: Association of American Colleges and Universities.

Zlotkowski, E., Horowitz, K., & Benson, S. (2011). The potential of service-learning student leadership. In N. V. Longo & C. M. Gibson (Eds.), *From command to community: A new approach to leadership education* (pp. 45–64). Medford, MA: Tufts University Press.

WENDY WAGNER *is an assistant professor of nonprofit and integrative studies and director of Community Engagement for Social Action & Integrative Learning (SAIL) in New Century College at George Mason University.*

PATRICIA MATHISON *is associate director of Social Action & Integrative Learning (SAIL) in New Century College at George Mason University.*

Formative assessment can be a critical and creative practice in leadership education and significantly enhance student learning, leader development, and leadership development. This chapter seeks to frame the use of assessment as both a best practice in leadership education and as an integral component to effective leadership learning pedagogy.

Formative Assessment as an Effective Leadership Learning Tool

J. Matthew Garrett, Jill M. Camper

Effective assessment practices are now seen as instrumental to demonstrating student learning and development, as well as to improving and justifying programs and services. Until the last decade, however, assessment on college campuses was infrequent and almost always involved a daunting process that was seen as added work (Bresciani, Moore, & Hickmott, 2009; Upcraft & Schuh, 1996). Nonetheless, assessment is viewed as integral to effective leadership pedagogy and program design. Although assessment is most often viewed as a learning tool for administrators to understand and improve the programs and services they provide, this utilitarian view of assessment hinders practitioners from capitalizing on its full pedagogical usefulness. This chapter seeks to reframe the use of assessment as both a best practice in leadership education and as an integral component to effective leadership learning pedagogy (Shutt, Garrett, Lynch, & Dean, 2012).

Assessment should be a core component of any effective leadership curriculum, and the information gleaned from assessment should be used to enhance student leadership learning, leadership self-efficacy, realistic self-appraisal, and many other key leadership learning outcomes (Ambrose, Bridges, DiPietro, Lovett, & Norman, 2010). Chapter 1 in this volume reviews a variety of national standards and guidelines for developing and assessing leadership programs and describes the call for more purposeful, comprehensive, and useful assessments of leadership programs (Roberts, 2007). When practitioners design programs that creatively integrate assessment as a student learning tool, they advance leadership programming in meaningful and significant ways.

NEW DIRECTIONS FOR STUDENT LEADERSHIP, no. 145, Spring 2015 © 2015 Wiley Periodicals, Inc., A Wiley Company
Published online in Wiley Online Library (wileyonlinelibrary.com) • DOI: 10.1002/yd.20127

Understanding Formative and Summative Assessment

Assessment is any effort undertaken to collect data about the effectiveness of a program or service, and then the act of using the data to improve a curriculum, change a service, demonstrate accomplishment of an outcome, or simply justify resource allocation (Upcraft & Schuh, 1996). Often administrators rely on pretest/posttest designs or focus groups to understand the broad picture of student learning that occurred by the end of a program. This is considered *summative* assessment (Bresciani et al., 2009). At the end of the experience, how did students change? Summative assessment is an important and necessary component of any effective assessment plan; however, summative assessment is not holistically sufficient to gauge leadership learning.

Conducted during a program or service, *formative* assessment is useful in improving learning or teaching while it is still occurring. As the saying goes, formative assessment is when the cook tastes the soup, and summative assessment is when the customer tastes the soup. Formative assessment, by nature, pushes educators to be more responsive to student learning during an educational experience (Ambrose et al., 2010). Unfortunately, most often formative assessments are simple check-ins throughout a program perhaps using various feedback methods such as a survey. However, many creative curricular and cocurricular activities exist through which formative assessments can be conducted to measure and intentionally focus on learning as it is happening.

Truly intentional formative assessments are centered on the learner, gather mutually beneficial information to both educator and student, and are designed to be specific and unique to that particular experience (Shutt et al., 2012). For example, the Emerging Leader Experience at Emory University uses a formative assessment to collect data about its effectiveness that then informs follow-up sessions (http://www.osls.emory.edu/programs /emerging_leader/index.html). Those data are also shared back with students in various ways that help the student see their own personal change as a result of the curriculum.

Formative assessment is most effective when it is used as a feedback tool to student participants and when administrators are responsive to those results (Angelo & Cross, 1993). Thus, formative assessments can take leadership education to a deeper level because this type of assessment is more focused on the developmental learning needs of the student participants.

Formative assessment is, at its core, a feedback tool, and feedback is a vital component in effective student learning techniques. Defined as information that is given to a person about his or her own performance that guides future behavior, feedback is an effective experiential learning technique (Ambrose et al., 2010). Scholarship exists that emphasizes the important role of experiential learning in leadership development (see Chapter 6 in this volume), and having multiple sources of feedback to provide an individual with a complete picture of how they are being perceived and how effective they are is vital to increasing both capacity and efficacy in leaders (e.g., Day, Harrison, & Halpin, 2009). One effective type of feedback is a 360-degree tool where a leader is able to get individual feedback from every direction, or 360 degrees, in an organization (Alimo-Metcalfe, 1998). This includes supervisors/advisors, peers/colleagues, and any members that may identify as followers or supervisees. An example of using 360-degree feedback with student leaders is offered at the end of this chapter.

To put theory into practice, consider this illustration. Educators know that in order to effect change leaders must be able to work positively and collaboratively with others. This leadership skill set is directly connected to an individual's consciousness of self in the social change model of leadership development (Higher Education Research Institute [HERI], 1996). As such, feedback is integral to the development of a realistic sense of self which will promote more effective collaboration and ultimately produce more effective leaders.

Many leadership educators conduct meaningful midintervention assessments, yet fail to incorporate the data back into the curriculum. This incorporation is what makes the assessment truly formative. Formative assessment becomes most effective when practitioners ask, "How can I use this data to provide meaningful feedback to *both* the students participating in the program and other decision makers?" instead of asking "how will I as an administrator use the data I collect?" This dual audience, of both students and decision makers, helps leadership educators develop curriculum that will be more effective for their students while also gathering important data necessary to justify and improve programs.

The reverse is also true. Many strong curricula across the country already have formative assessments embedded that are only used as a learning tool in the curriculum, when instead this valuable data could also be used for external purposes. Leadership educators should develop meaningful assessments by asking, "How will our students use the data to advance their own learning?". For example, when developing the Creating Emory initiative at Emory University (a leadership and bystander intervention program), practitioners started with the outcome for the programs and then developed creative assessment techniques, asking questions about how students would use data before writing the curriculum. What resulted was a highly effective inclusive leadership program where students used data about themselves and others to identify methods to individually contribute to building positive community at Emory.

Key Considerations in Designing Formative Assessments of Leadership Learning

When developing a leadership curriculum, educators should follow the advice of Stephen Covey (1989) and begin with the end in mind. Not only must a leadership educator begin with the ideal learning outcomes of the program (the end), the next step is considering how the outcomes would be most effectively assessed. This process provides clarity about *what* students are learning, and also about *how* educators can prove that students are learning. This is where educators can become creative in how they think about the connection of assessment with curriculum design.

Several key considerations in thinking about how to develop formative assessments of leadership learning include the thoughtful development of a common language of leadership, self-awareness of the learner, leadership self-efficacy, and an increasingly complex leadership identity.

Common Language.   Unifying the approach a campus takes to leadership development is helpful for students to make meaning of their leadership experiences across programs and services (Hannum, Martineau, & Reinelt, 2006). In order to develop an effective and comprehensive assessment strategy for a campus or even an office, a shared leadership vocabulary becomes important. A shared vocabulary can result in a congruent curriculum and collaborative assessment that may allow for deeper and more integrated student learning.

To develop a common language or approach to leadership development, it is important for practitioners to understand the differential effects of leader and leadership development programs for students with diverse identities (Guthrie, Bertrand Jones, Osteen, & Hu, 2013). When thinking about effective leader development, three important considerations arise (Day et al., 2009): building leader expertise or capacity, identity development of the individual, and adult development. Numerous theories can guide an approach to considering each of these important aspects (Guthrie et al., 2013). As a program transitions from focusing on individual leaders to instead developing abilities to influence and effect change in groups, organizations, and society, theories such as the social change model of leadership development (HERI, 1996) or the relational leadership model (Komives, Lucas, & McMahon, 2013) may prove helpful. These, too, can be adapted and considered for diverse student constituencies (Guthrie et al., 2013).

Self-Awareness.   The consideration of self-awareness throughout a leader development program should be a primary goal (Hannum et al., 2006). Self-awareness, further discussed in Chapters 2 and 5 of this volume, is fundamental to numerous leadership theories and underpins effective notions of emotional intelligence and leader development. Effective leader development programs will link leadership learning back to self, and formative assessments can be very helpful in accomplishing this goal. Specifically, feedback and coaching are directly linked to more realistic understandings of self (Day et al., 2009). Students should be encouraged to participate in facilitated activities where increased self-awareness and reflective judgment are core experiences (King & Kitchener, 1994).

Leadership Self-Efficacy.   The development of leadership self-efficacy is increasingly important in enhancing key leadership skills, especially those associated with developing an increasingly complex leadership identity (Komives, Longerbeam, Owen, Mainella, & Osteen, 2006). There are several ways to develop self-efficacy around any given subject matter. Mastery experiences, for example, are opportunities to have personal success at a given task (Bandura, 1995). Feedback on success of a task can support self-efficacy. Social persuasion comes when peers or mentors suggest to us that one does have what it takes to accomplish something, or positive feedback is given to promote confidence in the task (Bandura, 1995). These behaviors help develop efficacy, while critical feedback can, in some ways, hinder efficacy. Leadership educators should intentionally couple critical feedback with opportunities to incorporate the feedback and ultimately be successful at a given task to allow students to rebuild internal self-efficacy.

Leadership Identity Development.   Formative assessments can also be useful in helping student leaders develop an increasingly complex leadership identity (Komives et al., 2006). The leadership identity development (LID) model provides a framework practitioners can use to help move students from an internal sense of self where they do not view themselves as leaders to a sense of self where they not only see themselves as leaders, regardless of position, but also as able to effect change in a community or organization as a result of their skills. Formative assessments can provide key feedback for students to allow them to advance their personal view of self as leader.

Examples of Using Formative Assessment in Leadership Development

The Office of Student Leadership & Service (OSLS) at Emory University created a Leadership Steering Committee in 2010 (www.lead.emory.edu). Many of the outcomes, programs, and services at Emory use formative assessment and techniques discussed in this chapter to advance student leader and leadership development.

Common Language Identification: *Leadership Emory*.   In the spring of 2011, Leadership Emory was launched to situate Emory University as an institution innovatively enacting strategies to cultivate leadership within its entire student population. By boldly stating what the institution is trying to accomplish related to leadership, educators are able to more intentionally structure learning opportunities that connect to a common language and make leadership assessment more relevant. Comprised of five core tenets, Leadership Emory envisions the Emory student experience as the interconnection of cognitive complexity and the development of leadership capacities. Grounded in various key theoretical constructs such as the social change model of leadership development (HERI, 1996) and the relational leadership model (Komives et al., 2013), leadership is a process that is learned through extensive and ongoing training and reflection. The

Table 8.1   Leadership Emory Framework: Five Core Tenets of Leadership at Emory

Leadership Tenet	Description
Insight	Awareness of Self and Empathy With Others—Gain a deeper knowledge of self, success of personal endeavors, increased ability to establish relationships, and understand the values, interests, skills, and abilities of others
Integrity	Ethical Leadership Principles and Practices—Value clarification, understanding how values influence action, and ensuring those values are present in work with others.
Synergy	Collaboration and Problem Solving—Organizational leadership and effectiveness, managing others, creativity in problem solving, and other key group leadership tasks.
Purpose	Sharing the "Commitment to Action"—Establish buy-in from others, motivate others, share passions and ideas, and use support from others to help guide and shape a mutually shared vision.
Impact	Ethical Engagement and Citizenship—Support social justice work, giving back to the community, advocating equality and inclusiveness, and positively impacting others and society.

Source: Adapted from http://www.osls.emory.edu/leadership_emory/index.html

Leadership Emory tenets are developmental themes of leadership within which students will learn ideally for the rest of their lives. As students continue to explore each theme in deeper, more meaningful ways, they become more effective leaders.

The overarching goal is that by the time Emory students receive a diploma, they will have grown to embody the Five Core Tenets of Leadership at Emory (see Table 8.1).

The common language framework allows staff in Emory's Office of Student Leadership & Service to develop intentional leadership programs that make an impact. First, the creation of a common leadership language allows staff to develop comprehensive assessment instruments. Drawing on experts in the field as well as consulting on campus educators, scales to measure diverse facets of leadership were developed, tested, and refined over the course of three years. Now these scales can be used for any program with outcomes connected to Leadership Emory both as summative and formative assessment tools. Second, a qualitative instrument was developed and tested to gauge student learning more deeply relating to each of the tenets. Finally, the OSLS staff is in the process of developing rubrics for each of the 53 identified key outcomes of Leadership Emory. These rubrics have already been useful in making observations of student leaders in action and providing pointed feedback to support their development.

Developing Self-Awareness: *Summit Series.*   Using formative assessment to enhance self-awareness is a key part of the Leadership Emory

Summit Series. Each of the five core tenets (Impact, Insight, Purpose, Integrity, and Synergy) is featured in a day-long symposium that takes students through 10 hours of leadership curriculum.

Leadership assessment instruments are given to students when they register for the program. The data gathered through these pretests are used in two ways. First, use of pretest surveys helps program administrators to sort students into small groups based on level of preexposure to the outcomes. Beginner groups focus on different outcomes throughout the day than intermediate groups. For example, in the *Impact* program, participants experience a privilege walk. For beginner groups, the outcomes of small group debrief afterward focus on simple awareness of privilege. Outcomes for small groups that are more advanced focus on the implications of privilege to societal structures of oppression. This allows for students of all developmental levels to gain the most from a day-long curriculum.

A second use formative assessment tools to help students gain self-awareness around their level of development is with the *Insight* summit that focuses on self-awareness and emotional intelligence. Here students are given their pretests during a midday reflection. With feedback from their small group leaders, students do a midpoint reflection on their own leadership development and self-awareness. Finally, for all programs, the assessment instrument is administered again at the end of the program. This allows for a summative use of the data to look at participant outcome achievement throughout the entire program.

In the *Purpose* summit, students learn about developing a group vision for effecting positive change in a student organization and the Emory community. Throughout the day, students learn about developing a vision; however, they start the day with writing a vision statement with no coaching, information, or experience. At the end of the day, final drafts of vision statements are compared with the first drafts and coded by a peer and the small group facilitator using a rubric. This information is then provided to the student who reflects on what they have learned that day related to vision casting. This provides immediate formative assessment to enhance student learning and efficacy, and then the rubrics are used to evaluate the program in a summative way.

In the *Integrity* summit, students take assessments that examine their values. These assessments are collected and a map of all the values present in the group is created by the logistics coordinator. During lunch, a discussion about the group's values ensues, and participants compare their own values to those of the institution. This reflection is then discussed in small groups for students to share and receive feedback about their values structures. The reflection is then turned in, with specific information about how students see their values differently, and staff code the reflection to look for themes related to learning outcomes.

To be effective in group settings and to handle conflict effectively, student leaders must know how to give and receive feedback. In the *Synergy* summit, learning to give feedback is a core outcome. Throughout the day, peers interact with one another and are asked to take notes on their peers in their small groups. That afternoon, a session of peer-to-peer feedback occurs and small group facilitators observe students giving feedback. Using a rubric, they then have individual follow-up meetings and the student ends the day by crafting a personal mission statement for their style of giving feedback to peers in a group. These assessment data are again used formatively to provide students feedback in the moment and summatively to help prove learning outcome achievement.

Building Self-Efficacy: *Leadership Coaching.*   Coaching and mentorship are important and effective tools to consider using in leader development programs (Campbell, Smith, Dugan, & Komives, 2012). These types of programs allow students to receive individualized feedback that directly influences sense of self, self-awareness, efficacy, and identity. Although coaching programs can be time intensive and difficult to execute, Emory University launched a one-on-one coaching pilot program in 2014 that will be expanded in 2015. Using predeveloped assessment instruments, students participate in a 360-degree assessment where two peers, a faculty member or advisor, and the student, complete the assessment. Information is then compiled and students have an individual meeting with a member of the OSLS staff. During this meeting, further follow-up learning opportunities are discussed that address individual student's challenge areas.

Students are able to get feedback in real time which is most valuable so students, in the moment, can see how feedback connects to their actual behaviors and then have the chance to practice modified behavior. Then if students participate more than once (no more regularly than once per semester), their change over time is also analyzed and discussed. This program is being refined further so that it can be formally incorporated into formal staff trainings for orientation leaders, Volunteer Emory staff, and other leadership positional programs in the office.

Enhancing Leadership Identity Development: *Emerging Leaders.* The Emerging Leader Experience is a program with curriculum built on the foundations of the LID model (Komives et al., 2006). The primary goal is to develop a strong sense of awareness of leadership through each of the Five Core Tenets of Leadership Emory. One activity for students occurs when they first arrive at the retreat site. Students begin each session with a large sheet of paper and trace one another and then are asked to creatively represent what they think of when they imagine a leader. Students then participate in a series of activities that help them redefine leader, leadership, and self in context. The evening concludes with a deep discussion on the *Impact* tenet, which relates to inclusive leadership and the role of leaders to challenge systems of oppression. The final small group activity for the night is for students to redraw their pictures of attributes of a leader. Students then are given sticky notes to go around and quietly give one another feedback. On the final day, students are led through a series of individual reflections on confidence as a leader (efficacy) and identity as a leader to arrive at a final personal leadership identity mission statement. This formative peer assessment gives students real-time feedback throughout the retreat and then provides staff members with rich qualitative data to code for purposes of a final summative assessment report.

Conclusion

The opportunity exists to be creative, thoughtful, and even have fun when designing curriculum that includes formative assessments. Angelo and Cross (1993) provide a framework many leadership educators have found helpful in determining various dimensions of learning to assess, and Owen (2011) adapted their dimensions to provide various creative assessment techniques that may apply directly to leadership learning. In order to advance the effectiveness and impact of leadership development, educators must intentionally use assessments to both demonstrate the success of programs and to directly influence the development of the leader. Data gathered by leadership educators are too useful for individual leader development to allow them to sit unused on a shelf or in an unread report. The more leadership educators commit to gathering and using formative data for student development and leadership learning, the bigger difference we will make fostering socially responsible leadership in students and the world.

References

Alimo-Metcalfe, B. (1998). 360 degree feedback and leadership development. *International Journal of Selection and Assessment, 6*(1), 35–44.

Ambrose, S. A., Bridges, M. W., DiPietro, M., Lovett, M. C., & Norman, M. K. (2010). *How learning works: Seven research-based principles for smart teaching.* San Francisco, CA: Jossey-Bass.

Angelo, T. A., & Cross, K. P. (1993). *Classroom assessment techniques: A handbook for college teachers.* San Francisco, CA: Jossey-Bass.

Bandura, A. (1995). *Self-efficacy in changing societies.* London, UK: Cambridge University Press.

Bresciani, M. J., Moore Gardner, M., & Hickmott, J. (2009). *Demonstrating student success: A practical guide to outcomes-based assessment of learning and development in student affairs.* Sterling, VA: Stylus.

Campbell, C. M., Smith, M., Dugan, J. P., & Komives, S. R. (2012). Mentors and college student leadership outcomes: The importance of position and process. *The Review of Higher Education, 35,* 595–625.

Covey, S. R. (1989). *The seven habits of highly effective people: Restoring the character ethic.* New York, NY: Free Press.

Day, D. V., Harrison, M. M., & Halpin, S. M. (2009). *An integrative approach to leader development: Connecting adult development, identity, and expertise.* New York, NY: Routledge.

Guthrie, K. L., Bertrand Jones, T., Osteen, L., & Hu, S. (2013). *Cultivating leader identity and capacity in students from diverse backgrounds.* (ASHE Higher Education Report, 39[4]). San Francisco, CA: Jossey-Bass.

Hannum, K., Martineau, J. W., & Reinelt, C. (Eds.). (2006). *The handbook of leadership development evaluation*. San Francisco, CA: Wiley.

Higher Education Research Institute (HERI). (1996). *A social change model of leadership development* (Version III). Los Angeles: Higher Education Research Institute, University of California Los Angeles.

King, P. M., & Kitchener, K. S. (1994). *Developing reflective judgment: Understanding and promoting intellectual growth and critical thinking in adolescents and adults*. San Francisco, CA: Jossey-Bass.

Komives, S. R., Longerbeam, S. D., Owen, J. E., Mainella, F. C., & Osteen, L. (2006). A leadership identity development model: Applications from a grounded theory. *Journal of College Student Development, 47*, 401–418.

Komives, S. R., Lucas, N., & McMahon, T. R. (2013). *Exploring leadership: For college students who want to make a difference* (3rd ed.). San Francisco, CA: Jossey-Bass.

Owen, J. E. (2011). Considerations of student learning in leadership. In S. R. Komives, J. P. Dugan, J. E. Owen, C. Slack, W. Wagner, & Associates (Eds.), *The handbook for student leadership development* (2nd ed., pp. 109–133). San Francisco, CA: Jossey-Bass.

Roberts, D. C. (2007). *Deeper learning in leadership: Helping college students find the potential within*. San Francisco, CA: Jossey-Bass.

Shutt, M. S., Garrett, J. M., Lynch, J. L., & Dean, L. A. (2012). A model for identifying best practices. *Journal for Student Affairs Research & Practice, 1*(49), 65–82.

Upcraft, M. L., & Schuh, J. H. (1996). *Assessment in student affairs: A guide for practitioners*. San Francisco, CA: Jossey-Bass.

J. MATTHEW GARRETT *serves as the assistant dean for campus life and director of the Office of Student Leadership & Service at Emory University in Atlanta, Georgia.*

JILL M. CAMPER *serves as the associate director for leadership education and student life in the Office of Student Leadership & Service at Emory University in Atlanta, Georgia.*

Index

ORDER FORM SUBSCRIPTION AND SINGLE ISSUES

DISCOUNTED BACK ISSUES:

Use this form to receive 20% off all back issues of *New Directions for Student Leadership*.
All single issues priced at **$23.20** (normally $29.00)

TITLE	ISSUE NO.	ISBN

Call 1-800-835-6770 or see mailing instructions below. When calling, mention the promotional code JBNND to receive your discount.

SUBSCRIPTIONS: (1 YEAR, 4 ISSUES)

☐ New Order   ☐ Renewal

U.S.	☐ Individual: $89	☐ Institutional: $342
CANADA/MEXICO	☐ Individual: $89	☐ Institutional: $382
ALL OTHERS	☐ Individual: $113	☐ Institutional: $416

Call 1-800-835-6770 or see mailing and pricing instructions below.
Online subscriptions are available at www.onlinelibrary.wiley.com

ORDER TOTALS:

Issue / Subscription Amount: $ _____

Shipping Amount: $ _____
(for single issues only – subscription prices include shipping)

Total Amount: $ _____

SHIPPING CHARGES:

First Item	$6.00
Each Add'l Item	$2.00

(No sales tax for U.S. subscriptions. Canadian residents, add GST for subscription orders. Individual rate subscriptions must be paid by personal check or credit card. Individual rate subscriptions may not be resold as library copies.)

BILLING & SHIPPING INFORMATION:

☐ **PAYMENT ENCLOSED:** *(U.S. check or money order only. All payments must be in U.S. dollars.)*

☐ **CREDIT CARD:** ☐ VISA ☐ MC ☐ AMEX

Card number _____ Exp. Date _____

Card Holder Name _____ Card Issue # _____

Signature _____ Day Phone _____

☐ **BILL ME:** *(U.S. institutional orders only. Purchase order required.)*

Purchase order # _____
Federal Tax ID 13559302 • GST 89102-8052

Name _____

Address _____

Phone _____ E-mail _____

Copy or detach page and send to: **John Wiley & Sons, One Montgomery Street, Suite 1000, San Francisco, CA 94104-4594**

Order Form can also be faxed to: **888-481-2665**

PROMO JBNND

Made in the USA
Lexington, KY
28 August 2016